Twentieth-Century Britain: A Very Short Introduction

VERY SHORT INTRODUCTIONS are for anyone wanting a stimulating and accessible way in to a new subject. They are written by experts, and have been published in more than 25 languages worldwide.

The series began in 1995, and now represents a wide variety of topics in history, philosophy, religion, science, and the humanities. Over the next few years it will grow to a library of around 200 volumes – a Very Short Introduction to everything from ancient Egypt and Indian philosophy to conceptual art and cosmology.

Very Short Introductions available now:

ANCIENT PHILOSOPHY
  Julia Annas
THE ANGLO-SAXON AGE
  John Blair
ANIMAL RIGHTS   David DeGrazia
ARCHAEOLOGY   Paul Bahn
ARCHITECTURE
  Andrew Ballantyne
ARISTOTLE   Jonathan Barnes
ART HISTORY   Dana Arnold
ART THEORY   Cynthia Freeland
THE HISTORY OF
  ASTRONOMY   Michael Hoskin
ATHEISM   Julian Baggini
AUGUSTINE   Henry Chadwick
BARTHES   Jonathan Culler
THE BIBLE   John Riches
BRITISH POLITICS
  Anthony Wright
BUDDHA   Michael Carrithers
BUDDHISM   Damien Keown
CAPITALISM   James Fulcher
THE CELTS   Barry Cunliffe
CHOICE THEORY
  Michael Allingham
CHRISTIAN ART   Beth Williamson
CLASSICS   Mary Beard and
  John Henderson
CLAUSEWITZ   Michael Howard
THE COLD WAR
  Robert McMahon

CONTINENTAL PHILOSOPHY
  Simon Critchley
COSMOLOGY   Peter Coles
CRYPTOGRAPHY
  Fred Piper and Sean Murphy
DADA AND SURREALISM
  David Hopkins
DARWIN   Jonathan Howard
DEMOCRACY   Bernard Crick
DESCARTES   Tom Sorell
DRUGS   Leslie Iversen
THE EARTH   Martin Redfern
EGYPTIAN MYTHOLOGY
  Geraldine Pinch
EIGHTEENTH-CENTURY
  BRITAIN   Paul Langford
THE ELEMENTS   Philip Ball
EMOTION   Dylan Evans
EMPIRE   Stephen Howe
ENGELS   Terrell Carver
ETHICS   Simon Blackburn
THE EUROPEAN UNION
  John Pinder
EVOLUTION
  Brian and Deborah Charlesworth
FASCISM   Kevin Passmore
THE FRENCH REVOLUTION
  William Doyle
FREUD   Anthony Storr
GALILEO   Stillman Drake
GANDHI   Bhikhu Parekh

GLOBALIZATION
  Manfred Steger
HEGEL   Peter Singer
HEIDEGGER   Michael Inwood
HINDUISM   Kim Knott
HISTORY   John H. Arnold
HOBBES   Richard Tuck
HUME   A. J. Ayer
IDEOLOGY   Michael Freeden
INDIAN PHILOSOPHY
  Sue Hamilton
INTELLIGENCE   Ian J. Deary
ISLAM   Malise Ruthven
JUDAISM   Norman Solomon
JUNG   Anthony Stevens
KANT   Roger Scruton
KIERKEGAARD
  Patrick Gardiner
THE KORAN   Michael Cook
LINGUISTICS   Peter Matthews
LITERARY THEORY
  Jonathan Culler
LOCKE   John Dunn
LOGIC   Graham Priest
MACHIAVELLI
  Quentin Skinner
MARX   Peter Singer
MATHEMATICS
  Timothy Gowers
MEDIEVAL BRITAIN
  John Gillingham and
  Ralph A. Griffiths
MODERN IRELAND
  Senia Pašeta
MOLECULES   Philip Ball
MUSIC   Nicholas Cook
NIETZSCHE   Michael Tanner
NINETEENTH-CENTURY
  BRITAIN   Christopher Harvie and
  H. C. G. Matthew
NORTHERN IRELAND
  Marc Mulholland

PAUL   E. P. Sanders
PHILOSOPHY   Edward Craig
PHILOSOPHY OF SCIENCE
  Samir Okasha
PLATO   Julia Annas
POLITICS   Kenneth Minogue
POSTCOLONIALISM
  Robert Young
POSTMODERNISM
  Christopher Butler
POSTSTRUCTURALISM
  Catherine Belsey
PREHISTORY   Chris Gosden
PRESOCRATIC PHILOSOPHY
  Catherine Osborne
PSYCHOLOGY   Gillian Butler and
  Freda McManus
QUANTUM THEORY
  John Polkinghorne
ROMAN BRITAIN
  Peter Salway
ROUSSEAU   Robert Wokler
RUSSELL   A. C. Grayling
RUSSIAN LITERATURE
  Catriona Kelly
THE RUSSIAN REVOLUTION
  S. A. Smith
SCHIZOPHRENIA
  Chris Frith and Eve Johnstone
SCHOPENHAUER
  Christopher Janaway
SHAKESPEARE   Germaine Greer
SOCIAL AND CULTURAL
  ANTHROPOLOGY
  John Monaghan and Peter Just
SOCIOLOGY   Steve Bruce
SOCRATES   C. C. W. Taylor
SPINOZA   Roger Scruton
STUART BRITAIN
  John Morrill
TERRORISM   Charles Townshend
THEOLOGY   David F. Ford

Available soon:

For more information visit our web site
www.oup.co.uk/vsi

Kenneth O. Morgan

TWENTIETH-CENTURY BRITAIN

A Very Short Introduction

OXFORD
UNIVERSITY PRESS

OXFORD
UNIVERSITY PRESS

Great Clarendon Street, Oxford OX2 6DP

Oxford University Press is a department of the University of Oxford.
It furthers the University's objective of excellence in research, scholarship,
and education by publishing worldwide in

Oxford New York

Auckland Bangkok Buenos Aires Cape Town Chennai
Dar es Salaam Delhi Hong Kong Istanbul Karachi Kolkata
Kuala Lumpur Madrid Melbourne Mexico City Mumbai Nairobi
São Paulo Shanghai Taipei Tokyo Toronto

Oxford is a registered trade mark of Oxford University Press
in the UK and in certain other countries

Published in the United States
by Oxford University Press Inc., New York

Text © Kenneth O. Morgan 2000

Text first published in *The Oxford Illustrated History of Britain* 1984
First published as a Very Short Introduction 2000

British Library Cataloguing in Publication Data
Data available

Library of Congress Cataloging in Publication Data
Data available

ISBN 978-0-19-285397-4

9 10

Typeset by RefineCatch Ltd, Bungay, Suffolk
Printed in Italy by
Legoprint S.p.A., Lavis (TN)

Contents

List of Illustrations   viii

List of Maps   x

1   The First World War   1

2   The Twenties   15

3   The Thirties   31

4   The Second World War   45

5   The Post-War World   61

6   From the Seventies to the Nineties   79

7   Towards the Millennium   95

Further Reading   111

Chronology   115

Prime Ministers 1914–2000   119

Index   120

List of Illustrations

1 Photograph of recruits to the army under the 'Derby scheme', Southwark Town Hall, autumn 1915 4
Courtesy of Hulton Getty

2 Lloyd George talking to Indian soldiers near Fricourt, on the Somme, September 1916 10
Courtesy of The Imperial War Museum

3 Cartoon portrait of the economist John Maynard Keynes by David Low, first published in the *New Statesman and Nation*, 28 October 1933 19
Courtesy of the *New Statesman*

4 Photograph of mass production on the assembly line at Morris Motors, Cowley, Oxford, 1929 27
Courtesy of Hulton Getty

5 (*Top*) Child evacuees arriving at Eastbourne, Sussex, at the outbreak of war in 1939; (*bottom*) child wearing a gas mask 46
Courtesy of Popperfoto (*top*) and Hulton Getty (*bottom*)

6 *Tube Shelter Perspective* by Henry Moore, 1941 55
Courtesy of The Tate Gallery
By permission of the Henry Moore Foundation

7 The Labour Cabinet under Attlee, 23 August 1945 62
Courtesy of Hulton Getty

8 Margaret Rutherford, Stanley Holloway, and Paul Dupuis in a scene from Ealing 'Studios' *Passport to Pimlico* (1949) 67
Courtesy of The National Film Archives/© Canal + Image UK

9 Start of the first march from Trafalgar Square to the government weapons research establishment in Aldermaston, Berkshire, April 1958 75
Courtesy of Popperfoto

10 The North Sea oil rig *Sea Quest* 89
Courtesy of Popperfoto

11 Mourners outside Kensington Palace prior to the funeral of Princess Diana, September 1997 107
Photo Martin Argles, © *The Guardian*

List of Maps

1 The retreat from empire, 1947–80 70–1

Chapter 1
The First World War

At the Lord Mayor of London's annual banquet at the Mansion House on 17 July 1914, the chancellor of the Exchequer, David Lloyd George, issued stern warnings about the ominous condition of British society. At home, the 'triple alliance' of miners, railwaymen, and transport workers was threatening a mass united strike to back up the railwaymen's claim for union recognition and a 48-hour week. Alongside this prospect of nationwide industrial paralysis, there was across the Irish Sea a state of near civil war in Ireland, with 200,000 or more under arms in Protestant Ulster and the Catholic south, and the likelihood of the age-long saga of Irish nationalism being brought to a grim and bloody resolution. Abroad, there were nationalist troubles in India and in Egypt. Nearer home in south-east Europe, the ethnic nationalities of the Balkans were in renewed turmoil following the assassination of the Austrian archduke, Franz Ferdinand, at Sarajevo in Bosnia on 28 June.

On the eve of world war, therefore, Britain seemed to present a classic picture of a civilized liberal democracy on the verge of dissolution, racked by tensions and strains with which its sanctions and institutions were unable to cope. And yet, as so often in the past, once the supreme crisis of war erupted, these elements of conflict subsided with remarkable speed. An underlying mood of united purpose gripped the nation. The first few weeks of hostilities, after Britain declared war on 4 August, were, inevitably, a time of some panic. Only dramatic measures by the Treasury and the Bank of England preserved the national currency and credit. Manufacturing and commerce tried desperately to adjust to the challenges of war against the background of an ethic that proclaimed that it was 'business as usual'. The early experiences of actual fighting were almost disastrous as the British Expeditionary Force, cobbled together in much haste and dispatched to Flanders and France, met with a severe reverse at Ypres, and had to retreat from Mons, in disarray and suffering heavy losses. Reduced to only three corps in strength, its fighting force was gravely diminished almost from the start. Only a stern resistance by the French forces on the river Marne prevented a rapid German advance on Paris and an early victory for Germany and its Austrian allies.

After the initial disasters, however, the nation and its leaders settled down for a long war. Vital domestic issues such as Irish home rule were suspended for the duration of hostilities. The political parties declared an indefinite truce. The industrial disturbances of the summer of 1914 petered out, with the TUC outdoing the employers in voicing the conventional patriotism of the time. A curious kind of calm descended, founded on a broad – though very far from universal – consensus about the justice of the war. The one element required to make it acceptable to a liberal society was some kind of broad, humane justification to explain what the war was really about. This was provided by Lloyd George, once a bitter opponent of the Boer War in South Africa in 1899, and for many years the most outspokenly left-wing member of Asquith's Liberal government. Lloyd George remained suspiciously silent during the early weeks. But in an eloquent address to a massed audience of his Welsh fellow-countrymen at the Queen's Hall, London, on 19 September 1914, he committed himself without reserve to a fight to the finish. He occupied, or claimed to occupy, the highest moral ground. It was, he declared, a war on behalf of liberal principles, a crusade on behalf of the 'little five-foot-five nations', like Belgium, flagrantly invaded by the Germans, or Serbia and Montenegro, now threatened by Austria-Hungary. It was not surprising that a claim that the war was a holy cause, backed up not only by the leaders of all the Christian Churches but by all the Liberal pantheon of heroes from Charles James Fox to Gladstone, met with instant response, not least in the smaller nations of Scotland and Wales within Britain itself.

Pro-War Consensus

This broad consensus about the rightness of the war was not fundamentally eroded over the next four terrible years. Of course, it went through many changes, especially after the unpopular decision to impose conscription for the armed services was instituted in May 1916. Eventually, by 1917, sheer war-weariness was taking its toll, quite apart from other factors such as the growing militancy from organized labour and the Messianic appeal of the Bolshevik revolution in Russia. Of course, too, this consensus was sustained by subtle or crude manipulation of the news services, censorship of the press, and government-sponsored legends of atrocities allegedly committed by 'the Huns'. There was much persecution of radical or anti-war critics. In spite of government pressures, bodies such as the Christian pacifist 'No-Conscription Fellowship' and the Union of Democratic Control (which sought a negotiated peace) were by 1917 making some impact on public opinion. Lord Lansdowne's appeal for peace (29 November 1917) caused a great stir. Nevertheless, the available evidence for the war years suggests that the broad mass of the population retained its faith that the war was just and necessary, and that it must be fought until the total surrender of the German enemy, whatever the cost. Recruitment to the armed services from volunteers was heavy and enthusiastic: indeed voluntary recruitment proved more successful in swelling the ranks of the army in France in 1914–16 than was the compulsory method of conscription thereafter. The long years of military and naval conflict that dragged on from the initial stalemate on the western front in the autumn of 1914, until the final Allied breakthrough in August–September 1918 were accepted with resignation and a kind of grim endurance.

1. Recruits to the army under the 'Derby scheme', Southwark Town Hall, autumn 1915. In October 1915, Lord Derby introduced a scheme designed to preserve the voluntary recruitment system by allowing men to register to 'attest' their willingness to serve. Popular enthusiasm remained extremely high: 235,000 men volunteered under the Derby scheme in October–November 1915. But universal male conscription duly followed in early 1916

The psychological and moral impact of those appalling years sank deep into the memory and the outlook of the British people. They profoundly coloured the literary sensibilities of a whole generation. They helped shape responses to the threat of foreign war for twenty years after the Great War came to an end. The war on the western front took the unfamiliar form of a prolonged slogging match between heavily defended forces on either side, dug into slit trenches, and unable to exploit the new techniques of mobile striking power so dramatically tested in the Franco-Prussian war of 1870. For almost four years, the war in France showed little movement. There were occasional British attempts to seize the initiative. Always they ended in huge casualties on a scale scarcely comprehensible to a nation which lived on the luxurious memories of a century of almost unbroken peace. The British offensive at Loos was beaten back in September 1915. More damaging still, in June 1916 a new British advance on the Somme proved a calamitous failure with 60,000 men falling on the first day. British casualties here alone amounted to 420,000. The most terrible of these experiences came at Passchendaele in August–September 1917, when over 300,000 British troops were recorded as dead or wounded, many of them drowned in the mud of Flanders amidst torrential rain. Both the cavalry and mechanical inventions such as the 'tanks' made no impact in so immobile a campaign. The new fighter aircraft had little effect. As on other occasions, the class divide that cut off commanding officers from the rank-and-file infantrymen and hindered communication between them was fatal throughout. In effect, the British ceased to be a viable offensive force for the next few months. March and April 1918 saw the British army desperately striving to ward off a new German advance in the Amiens sector. Nor until the ultimate dramatic breakthrough by the commander-in-chief Sir Douglas Haig that August did the war show signs of coming to a resolution. Meanwhile attempts, advocated by Lloyd George and Winston Churchill amongst others, to circumvent the stalemate on the western front by a more peripheral 'eastern' strategy also led to successive débâcles. The Dardanelles expedition in the summer of 1915 was a colossal exercise in military mismanagement and led to further huge losses; so did the expedition to Salonika a year later. The Dardanelles in particular did immense harm to Churchill's reputation as a rational politician, from which he took years to recover. Even on the high seas, Britain's traditional area of supremacy, the one major battle, the encounter off Jutland in June 1916, was at best a draw between the British and German high fleets. The British Grand Fleet lost three battle cruisers, three other cruisers, and eight destroyers in an ill-conducted engagement.

Later anti-war propaganda depicted an angry populace displaying fierce hostility towards the military and naval commanders responsible for this terrible catalogue of disaster in almost every theatre. 'War poets' such as Wilfred Owen and Isaac Rosenberg (who fell in battle) and

Siegfried Sassoon and Robert Graves (who survived), stirred particularly by the carnage of Passchendaele, all encouraged the view that a mass renunciation took place of the very idea of war itself, of the carnage that could result in half an entire generation of young men being wiped out. The bare statistics of the war – 750,000 killed, another 2,500,000 wounded, many permanently disabled – reinforced this belief in a mass rejection of militarism. That was not, however, how it appeared to most people at the time, even if it should have done so. While the British commander-in-chief on the western front, Sir John French, was indeed removed from command at the end of 1915, his successor, Haig, a grim, taciturn Lowland Scot, steadily built up a massive public reputation for courage and integrity, a reputation matched by Sir Edwin Lutyens's towering war memorial to commemorate the British dead at Thiepval. Other naval and military leaders, such as Admiral Beatty and General Allenby (who conducted a brilliant campaign from Egypt, through Palestine into Syria in 1917–18, to eliminate the Turks as significant allies for the Germans), became almost popular heroes. The trenches became the symbol of stern, but inescapable, resolution. Bruce Bairnsfather's famous cartoon of 'Old Bill', urging his comrade that if he knew of 'a better 'ole' he should go to it, symbolized a popular mood of almost humorous tolerance of the terrors of trench warfare. When, after desperate military crises and with the immense military and financial aid of the United States, the British and French armies forced their way through the German lines to reach the borders of Germany itself by the time of the armistice on 11 November 1918, mass enthusiasm for the war appeared at its zenith. Britain seemed in danger of inventing a new military cult unknown in these islands since the days of Marlborough in the reign of Queen Anne.

Total War

A major factor in the widespread popularity of the war – and also in its subsequent bitter unpopularity – was the involvement of the whole population and the entire social and economic fabric in total war. After a leisurely start, in 1915–16 the war brought about a massive industrial and social transformation; it erected a leviathan of state power and collectivist control without precedent. The forces of production and distribution in industry and agriculture were all harnessed to fuel the needs of a mighty war machine. The model was set by the new Ministry of Munitions of which Lloyd George assumed control in May 1915. Created to deal with bottle-necks in the supply of arms and ammunition, the ministry became the engine of a massive central machine which invigorated the entire industrial structure through its 'men of push and go'. It achieved an immense impact as well on such different areas as social welfare, housing policy, and the status of women. The coal mines, the railways, and merchant and other shipping were all taken under State control. The old pre-war shibboleths of *laissez-faire*, including the hallowed principle of free trade itself, were bypassed or ignored. Equally, the traditional system of industrial relations was wrenched into totally new patterns. The Treasury Agreement of March 1915, negotiated between the government and the trade unions (except for the miners), forbade strikes but also guaranteed collective bargaining and, indirectly, a new access to government for trade union leaders.

The Treasury Agreement certainly did not achieve its aim of universal industrial peace during the war years. There were major disputes in the coal industry, notably a successful official strike by the South Wales Miners' Federation in July 1915. The work of the Ministry of Munitions in trying to 'dilute' the work-force by introducing unskilled workers (especially women) into engineering factories, and in trying to control the movements of labour in the armaments industry, brought much trouble, notably on Clydeside. The unofficial activities of shop stewards in Scotland and also in Sheffield in 1916–17 remind us that the consensus of the war years was a shallow one and very far from unanimous. Nevertheless, the war did ensure a continuing corporate status for the unions – and also for employers, newly combined in the Federation of British Industry. A new, organic, planned system of industrial relations

7

appeared to be possible. It was significant that powerful businessmen such as Sir Eric Geddes and Sir Joseph Maclay, Lord Devonport and Lord Rhondda, appeared in key departments of central government. This symbolized the transformation in the relationship of industrial and political leadership that was taking place. Edward VII's Liberal England was being turned into a corporate State, almost what a later generation would term 'Great Britain Limited'.

Social Reform

Over a vast range of social and cultural activities, the collective impact of the Great War was profound indeed. Left-wing opponents of the war, such as Ramsay MacDonald of the Labour Party, noted ironically that the imperatives of war were achieving far more for social reform than had all the campaigns of the trade unions and of progressive humanitarians in half a century past. New vistas of governmental activity were being opened up. Fresh layers were being added to the technocratic, professional, and civil service elite that had governed Britain in the years of peace. The administrative and managerial class expanded massively. Social reformers such as William Beveridge or Seebohm Rowntree, even the socialist Beatrice Webb, became influential and even honoured figures in the recesses of central government, especially after Lloyd George succeeded Asquith as prime minister in December 1916. Wages went up; working conditions improved. The 1917 Corn Production Act revitalized British agriculture and gave a fresh lease of life to tenant farmers and their labourers. Attention was also paid to technical and other education, notably through H. A. L. Fisher's act of 1918 which made free elementary education general and sought to create a ladder of opportunity from the elementary to the secondary and higher levels of education. Governmental inquiries, one of them headed by as conservative a figure as Lord Salisbury, opened up new vistas for state housing schemes, an area almost totally neglected by the New Liberalism before 1914. The principle was laid down for a system of subsidized local-authority houses, to provide the hundreds of thousands of working-class dwellings for rent that were required, and to remove the blight of slums in city centres and older industrial areas. Concern was voiced, too, for public health. The supreme irony was that a war which brought the loss of human life on such a colossal scale also saw the preservation of life at home through improved medical arrangements, better conditions for children, old people, and nursing mothers, and such innovations as the Medical Research Council. By the end of 1918, the government was committed to the idea of a new Ministry of Health to co-ordinate the services for health and national insurance, and to take over the duties of the Local Government Board.

Women

One important element of British society above all other gained from the wartime experience – indeed for them (a majority of the population, in fact) this was an era of emancipation. Women in Britain were supreme beneficiaries of the war years. Thousands of them served at the front, often in medical field hospitals. The spectacle of Nurse Edith Cavell martyred by the Germans for assisting in the escape of British and French prisoners of war in Belgium added powerfully to the public esteem of women in general. At home, suffragette leaders such as Mrs Emmeline Pankhurst and her elder daughter Christabel (though not her socialist younger daughter, Sylvia) aided in recruiting campaigns for the government. More widely, women found vast new opportunities in clerical and administrative work, in munitions and other engineering factories, and in many other unfamiliar tasks previously reserved for men only. The very dissolution wrought by total war exerted powerful pressures in eroding the sex barriers which had restricted British women over the decades. It was hardly possible to argue now that women were incapable of exercising the rights of citizenship to the full; in the 1918 Representation of the People Act, therefore, women aged 30 and over were given the vote. It was almost anti-climactic. A long, bitter saga of persecution and prejudice ended with a whimper. Here as elsewhere, by emphasizing the positive, progressive consequences of the war, with the full panoply of 'reconstruction' (ill-defined) which was supposed to be launched when peace returned, the government contrived, perhaps unintentionally, to extend and fortify the consensus of the time.

Politics

For British politics, the Great War produced massive and tumultuous changes. At the outbreak of war, the House of Commons was still largely dominated by the Gilbertian rivalry of Liberals and Conservatives (or Unionists). However, for the Liberal Party the war brought disaster. Partly this was because of the serious inroads into individual and civil liberties that war entailed. Partly it was due to a deep-seated ambiguity about the very merits of the war that many Liberals harboured. The

2. Lloyd George talking to Indian soldiers near Fricourt, on the Somme, September 1916. Both as secretary of State for war (July–December 1916) and as prime minister (from December 1916), Lloyd George projected his personal leadership by visits to soldiers on the front in France

turning of Asquith's Liberal administration into a three-party coalition in May 1915 marked a new stage in the downfall of Liberalism. Thereafter, Asquith's own apparently lethargic and fumbling leadership was accompanied by severe internal party divisions over the fundamental issue of military conscription. Lloyd George and Churchill both endorsed conscription as the symbol of whole-hearted commitment to 'a fight to the finish'. More traditional Liberals such as John Simon and Reginald McKenna were hesitant. Asquith himself dithered unhappily. In the end, conscription came for all adult males aged between 18 and 45, but criticism of Asquith and the Liberal ethic generally continued to mount.

In December 1916 the final crisis came. There had been complaints for months over government failures, not only in the field, but also over the inability to resolve the Irish question and to settle labour disputes at home. Between 1 and 9 December 1916 there followed political manoeuvres of Byzantine complexity over which historians continue to dispute like so many medieval schoolmen. Lloyd George joined with two leading Unionists, Bonar Law and the Irishman Sir Edward Carson, in proposing to Asquith a new supreme War Committee to run the war. After days of uncertainty, Asquith refused. Lloyd George then resigned and, in a crucial trial of strength between 4 and 9 December, emerged as prime minister of something like an all-party coalition. It included not only all the Unionists but also (by a very narrow majority on the National Executive) the Labour Party as well, in addition to roughly half the Liberals in the House of Commons. Henceforth, between December 1916 and November 1918, Lloyd George built himself up into a semi-presidential position of near impregnability. He was the prime minister of a supreme War Cabinet, backed up by a new Cabinet office and a 'garden suburb' or kitchen cabinet of private secretaries. Beneath this apex extended a mighty machine of centralized power. Lloyd George's triumph helped to win the war – but for his own Liberal Party it meant a débâcle. The party remained split, weakened at the grass roots, ineffective and divided in Parliament, shorn of much of its morale and impetus in the press and in intellectual circles. The New Liberalism, which had animated so much social reform before 1914, just spluttered out. When the war ended in November 1918, the Liberals were a divided, much weakened rump, a supreme casualty of total war.

Their place was taken, quite unexpectedly, by the Labour Party. This party had also been much divided by the outbreak of war. In contrast to the patriotism of trade union leaders, MacDonald and many on the socialist left had been opponents of entering the war. MacDonald had to resign his leadership of the parliamentary Labour Party in consequence. Issues during the war such as the impact of conscription (military and possible industrial), and the decision over whether or not to serve under Lloyd George, also plagued the Labour Party. Nevertheless, the long-term consequences of the war for the party were wholly beneficial. The trade unions on which Labour depended were much strengthened by the war experience. Their membership roughly doubled to reach over 8 million by the start of 1919. The party was also given new stimulus by the revolution in Russia, and by the wider anti-war radicalism in the last two years of the war. In effect, Labour was serving in government and acting as the formal Opposition at one and the same time. It was ideally placed to exploit the internal difficulties of the Liberals. Finally, the 1918 franchise reforms extended the electorate from about 8 million to over 21 million. This meant a huge increase in the working-class vote and an encouragement of the tendency to polarize politics on grounds of class. The 1918 party constitution gave the party a new socialist commitment and, more important, a reorganized structure in the constituencies and in Head Office, dominated throughout by the trade unions. The advance of Labour was a powerful political consequence of the war, though quite unforeseen at the time.

The real beneficiaries were the Conservatives. The war encouraged a process by which they became the natural majority party. Apart from being united by the call by war, as the patriots they claimed to be, after being divided over tariffs and other questions before 1914, the

Conservatives became increasingly dominated by business and manufacturing interests. They were now largely urban or suburban in their base, not a party of squires. At the end of the war, with new business-oriented figures such as Stanley Baldwin and Neville Chamberlain coming through, the Conservatives were poised, like the Labour Party, to destroy the Edwardian political system. When the war ended on 11 November 1918, Lloyd George assumed total command. His rump of Coalition Liberals were in electoral alliance with the Conservatives, in opposition to the 'pacifists' of the anti-government Liberals and the 'Bolsheviks' of the Labour Party. A new era of right-wing domination was in the making.

The British Empire

Externally, the war years encouraged further changes. It was, in all senses, a profoundly imperial war, fought for empire as well as for king and country. Much was owed to military and other assistance from Australia, New Zealand, Canada, South Africa, and India. Anzac Day (with memories of Suvla Bay, Gallipoli) became a tragic, symbolic event in the Australian calendar. In 1917 Lloyd George actually convened an Imperial War Cabinet of prime ministers to assist the Cabinet of the mother country. A powerful empire statesman like General Jan Smuts of South Africa was even called upon to participate in the deliberations of the British Cabinet. In commerce, imperial preference was becoming a reality. The imperial mystique was a powerful one at this time. The main architect of the day, Edwin Lutyens, had been in his younger days a disciple of the arts and crafts movement inspired by William Morris. Now he and Herbert Baker were turning their talents to pomp and circumstance by rebuilding the city of Delhi. It was to be dominated by a massive viceroy's residence and secretariat buildings as symbols of classical authority. During the war years, the imperial idea was taken further than ever before. Indeed, the secret treaties of the war years ensured that at the peace the mandate system or other stratagems would leave Britain with an imperial domain larger than ever, with vast

13

new territories in the Middle East and up from the Persian Gulf. Buoyed up by the eccentric operations of individualists such as 'Lawrence of Arabia' and fired by the heady prospects of vast oil riches in Mesopotamia and elsewhere in the Middle East, the bounds of the British Empire extended ever wider.

Yet in reality it was all becoming increasingly impractical to maintain. Long before 1914, the financial and military constraints upon an effective imperial policy were becoming clear, especially in India with its growing Congress movement. There was something else now – new and increasingly effective nationalist uprisings against British rule. Unlike Wales, which was almost mindlessly patriotic with Lloyd George at the helm, Ireland offered a disturbing spectacle of colonial revolt. The Easter Rising of April 1916, conducted by a few republicans and Sinn Fein partisans, seemed to be a fiasco. But, aided by the brutal reaction of Asquith's government, by mid-1918 Sinn Fein and its republican creed had won over almost all the 26 southern Irish counties. A veteran home ruler such as John Dillon was being swept aside by new nationalist radicals such as Michael Collins and Eamon de Valera. By the end of the war, southern Ireland was virtually under martial law, resistant to conscription, in a state of near rebellion against the Crown and the Protestant ascendancy, or what was left of it. The long march of Irish nationalism, constitutional and largely peaceful in the decades from Daniel O'Connell in the 1840s to Charles Stewart Parnell in the 1880s and John Redmond after 1900, seemed on the verge of producing a new and violent explosion. One clear moral of the war years, therefore, was that the political and social consensus, fragile enough for Clydeside and the Welsh mining valleys, did not extend at all to southern Ireland. With the powerful thrust of Irish republicanism, a new kind of nationalist revolt against the constraints of imperial rule was well under way. Indians and Egyptians, among others, were likely to pay careful heed. The war left a legacy of a more integrated but also a more isolated Britain, whose grandiose imperial role was already being swamped by wider transformations in the post-war world.

Chapter 2
The Twenties

When peace returned, it seemed that little had changed. The continuity between war and peace was confirmed by Lloyd George's overwhelming electoral triumph at the general election of December 1918, a ratification of the patriotism and unity of the war years. It was called 'the coupon election' because of the letter of endorsement given to candidates supporting the coalition. The prime minister was acclaimed, almost universally, as 'the man who won the war', the most dominant political leader since Oliver Cromwell. The electoral verdict was indeed an overpowering one. The supporters of the coalition government numbered no fewer than 526 (of whom 136 were Liberals and almost all the rest Unionists), against a mere 57 Labour MPs and 26 Independent Liberals. The results were not so conclusive under closer examination. The Labour Party's tally of 57 MPs concealed the fact that the party had polled two and a half million votes, and was on the verge of a massive electoral breakthrough. In Ireland, Sinn Fein captured 73 seats out of 81 in the south; its representatives withdrew from Westminster and set up their own unofficial parliament or 'Dáil' in Dublin. Even so, the mandate on behalf of the prime minister and his wartime associates seemed quite irrefutable.

The election seemed to confirm, too, that socio-economic normality in many respects was being rapidly restored. Many of the wartime controls and the apparatus of state collectivism disappeared as if they had never been. Major industries were returned to private hands – the railways, shipping, even the coal mines, whose owners were perhaps the most hated group in the entire capitalist world. The government also began a consistent financial policy to ensure an eventual return to the gold standard; this would entail a deflationary approach, with a steady contraction of the note issue expanded so rapidly during the war. The City of London, the class system, and private capitalism appeared destined to continue their unchallenged reign. To indicate that this was capitalism with a human face, the government also began with a flurry of reforming activity in 1919–20. Indeed, Lloyd George had campaigned far more vigorously at the election as a social reformer anxious to build a 'land fit for heroes' than as a chauvinist determined to hang the Kaiser or 'squeeze Germany till the pips squeaked'. So there followed a vigorous, if short-lived, programme to extend health and educational services, to raise pensions, and to spread universal unemployment insurance. Most spectacular of all was the subsidized housing programme launched by the Liberal minister, Dr Christopher Addison, which, with reluctant Treasury support, achieved a total of over 200,000 publicly built houses in the 1919–22 period, a limited but valuable start in dealing with one of the major social scandals in the land.

Economic and Political Problems

But it soon became disturbingly clear that life was not normal and that the comforting framework of pre-1914 could not easily be restored. There were new and disruptive economic problems that resulted from the loss of foreign markets and the sale of overseas investments to pay for the war. The most ominous aspect of this, on which newspaper headlines focused attention, was the huge increase in the national debt. The unredeemed capital of the debt stood at £706 million in 1914. Six years later it had soared to £7,875 million. This resulted in a passionate cry for 'economy', the ending of 'waste' in public expenditure, and a return to a balanced budget and a firm currency after the rapid inflation of 1918–19.

Politically, too, things were very far from normal. Lloyd George's coalition had come to power in unhappy circumstances, with a background of conspiracy surrounding the calling of the 1918 'coupon' general election. Its moral title to power was in doubt. Furthermore, as a coalition it was prey to internal disputes, and to constant tension between the Liberal prime minister and his Conservative colleagues over domestic, foreign, and imperial affairs. Lloyd George himself, a remote, Olympian figure, preoccupied with international peace conferences, aloof from the House of Commons, a prime minister without a party, an adventurer careless in his financial and sexual activities, was not one who inspired universal trust or affection. So the consensus of the armistice period soon evaporated and new conflicts took its place.

A series of challenges was launched which gradually undermined the coalition's claim to govern. New patterns were being formed which would shape the course of British history for the next twenty years. On the left, Lloyd George was bitterly attacked by many Liberals over his casualness towards old and hallowed principles such as free trade. His policy in Ireland appeared even more shocking, since the British government pursued war against the Irish Republican Army (IRA) in 1919–21 with an unrestrained policy of retaliation, which led to bloody atrocities being committed by the auxiliary forces that were maintained by the Crown to back up the army and the constabulary. In December 1921, Lloyd George, always by instinct a negotiator, eventually concluded a peace with the Sinn Fein leaders, Arthur Griffith and Collins. From January 1922, an Irish Free State, consisting of the 26 Catholic counties of southern Ireland, was created, with just the 6 Protestant counties of Ulster in the north-east left within the United Kingdom. But this *volte-face* was too late to repair Lloyd George's tarnished image amongst liberal opinion.

In the Labour and trade union world, the prime minister totally lost the reputation he had long enjoyed as a patron of labour. His government used tough methods, including emergency powers and the use of troops as strike-breakers, in dealing with national strikes by miners, railwaymen, and many other workers (including even the police) in 1919–21. Thereafter, the government failed to prevent massive unemployment (soon rising to over a million workers) from growing up and casting a blight over the older industrial areas. Episodes like the apparent deceiving of the coal-miners over the dropping of the Sankey report which had proposed the nationalization of the mines in 1919, and the further undermining of the 'Triple Alliance' to frustrate the miners again on 'Black Friday' (15 April 1921), sank deep into the consciousness of the working class. A government elected to promote national solidarity and social unity had made the class divide wider than ever before. If the coalition was attacked on the left, it was increasingly under fire on the right as well. Conservatives longed for the return of a healthy system of independent party politics, freed from the buccaneering methods of an autocratic prime minister and his retainers. Although the coalition hung on for almost four years, it was in dire straits and Lloyd George himself a prime minister at bay.

Above and beyond all this, there was a wider mood of disillusion with the peace treaties and the 'system of Versailles'. The 1919 peace settlement was increasingly unpopular. It was linked with secret treaties concluded during the war between Britain and its allies, and with unjust terms, for financial reparation and frontier arrangements, imposed on the defeated Germans. No book more effectively expressed this mood than did the economist J. M. Keynes's *Economic Consequences of the Peace* (1919). The work of a financial adviser to the Treasury who had resigned in protest during the Paris peace conference, it rapidly became a best seller on both sides of the Atlantic. It seemed to show conclusively that the reparations imposed on Germany would lead to its financial ruin and thereby to the permanent weakening of the European economy. Keynes also evoked, in memorable and picturesque language, the frenzied, corrupt atmosphere

J. M. Keynes

3. John Maynard Keynes, drawn here by David Low in a cartoon in the *New Statesman and Nation*, 28 October 1933, was the most influential economist of the twentieth century. *His General Theory* (1936) revolutionized ideas about economic theory and policy, while *Economic Consequences of the Peace* (1919) helped spread disillusion with the results of the First World War

in which the various covert bargains were struck by the peacemakers in Versailles. Lloyd George was condemned as a man 'rooted in nothing'. The premier's efforts to act as the peacemaker of Europe in successive international conferences became unpopular. Britain refused any longer to act, in Bonar Law's striking phrase, as 'the policeman of the world'. The empire might be larger than ever, but it must be accompanied by a withdrawal from commitments in Europe. Otherwise another tragedy would afflict the land as it had done in August 1914. The final blow for Lloyd George's coalition came in October 1922, when it seemed that Britain was on the verge of war with Turkey over the defence of the Greek position in Asia Minor and protection of the Straits. Conservatives as well as the British left revolted against this rekindling of jingoism. The right-wing basis of the government collapsed. Lloyd George fell from power on 19 October 1922, a political pariah for the rest of his life.

Two kinds of reaction against Lloyd George's government followed. They were symbolized respectively by MacDonald and Stanley Baldwin, both prominent in the movements that led to the downfall of the coalition in October 1922. MacDonald, with his heady utopian internationalism and 'Brave New World' idealism, was the perfect voice for the growing Labour Party, whose tally of seats rose rapidly in the 1922 and 1923 general elections. He could straddle the socialism of Clydeside and the social conventions of the London establishment. Alternatively, and more influential still, Baldwin led the Conservative forces of suburban middle-class respectability and of orthodox patriotism, all alarmed at Lloyd George's political experiments and the international adventurism of British foreign policy after the war. Baldwin, prime minister in 1923–4, 1924–9, and 1935–7, was an appropriate leader for a Britain desperate for a return to tranquillity and social peace.

Nationalism and the Arts

There was constant flux and upheaval in other spheres of public life as well. Many of the settled patterns of the pre-war period now seemed under assault. In Wales and Scotland there were small movements of intellectuals, which suggested that the very unity of the kingdom could itself be threatened. Two small nationalist parties were formed on the Irish model, Plaid Cymru in Wales in 1925 and the National Party of Scotland in 1928. However, their significance was to lie in a distant future.

In the arts, in literature, music, painting, and architecture, the surviving presence. of pre-war giants such as Rudyard Kipling and Thomas Hardy, Edward Elgar and Lutyens, masked the underlying challenge of avant-garde movements expressive of 'modernism' and revolt. Amongst the novelists, the main work of James Joyce and of D. H. Lawrence had already been written; indeed after *Women in Love* appeared in 1920, with its echoes of the *malaise* of the war years, Lawrence's later work seemed relatively unimpressive. More innovative were the writings of the coterie of intellectuals and artists linked with the 'Bloomsbury group'. In particular, the remarkable series of 'stream of consciousness' novels produced by Virginia Woolf, with their subtle delineation of human character and strangely fluid form, testified to the vitality of 'modernism' in the novel. More orthodox was E. M. Forster's *Passage to India* (1924), the work of a novelist indirectly associated with Bloomsbury, which, in its treatment of the interaction of Western and Eastern cultures, portrays the declining self-confidence of Western liberal humanism. The most notable pioneering development in poetry was T. S. Eliot's 'The Waste Land' (1922) with its disturbing rhythms and imagery; its pervading tone of Christian resignation and private melancholy captures one powerful aspect of the culture of the twenties. It was not a creative time for the theatre other than Bernard Shaw's *St Joan*, his most powerful philosophic affirmation. Nor was it an age of great imagination in art, design, and architecture either; painters like

Ben Nicholson were still seeking a new style, while others such as Paul Nash were apparently marking time. In the world of art, the Bloomsbury group again provided a few notable rebels, such as Roger Fry, the art critic and patron, and painters such as Duncan Grant and Vanessa Bell, trying to break out of the mould of realism in pictorial representation. Bloomsbury, indeed, with its writers and artists, and associated figures like the economist J. M. Keynes, the essayist Lytton Strachey, and its philosopher-mentor G. E. Moore, embodied many of the strengths and limitations of the British cultural scene in the twenties. It genuinely attempted to infuse British art with the inspiration of the modernist poets and surrealist artists of Continental Europe. It combined the cult of the new with an effective iconoclasm, most popularly conveyed in Strachey's satirical studies of the feet of clay of leading Victorian personalities, from the queen downwards. More negatively, Bloomsbury encouraged an inbred, almost tribal, view of artistic communication; it became in time a sheltered enclave with dynastic overtones. Writers in the thirties were to criticize the Bloomsbury group as a new cultural establishment. They attacked the group for laying insufficient emphasis on moral (rather than purely aesthetic) sensibility and for their supposed lack of political or public concern. Probably the Bloomsbury ethos encouraged a tendency for the art of the classes and masses to grow further and further apart.

Developments in the arts, however, with their expressions of revolt and emancipation, chimed in with wider social movements of the time. The women who gained the vote, partially in 1918 and then (conclusively) in 1928, were able to enjoy other freedoms as well: the right to smoke, to enjoy new leisure interests such as the films, to pursue a more open and less constrained 'sex life', and to wear clothes that were spectacularly less drab or puritanical. The 'bright young things' extolled in memoirs of the twenties, for whom the satires and plays of Noel Coward appeared to have been specifically written, were limited enough in their outlook. They were usually of middle- to upper-class background. They, or their friends, were strongly associated with the public schools, with

Oxford and Cambridge. Oxford, in particular, became linked with a kind of free cultural self-expression, tending to decadence, nihilism, or both, just as it was to be identified (equally wrongly) in the thirties with anti-war protest. The older universities were probably far less influential in society at large than later myth-mongers alleged, but they merged into the experimental climate of a more formless, rootless world.

The Churches

Certainly, the older arbiters of moral standards seemed to be suffering a crisis of authority after the war. Nowhere was this more apparent than amongst the Churches, manifestly among the casualties of total war, with the possible exception of the Roman Catholics with their strongly Irish membership. The nonconformist chapels, moral beacons to many in the Victorian heyday, were now suffering from falling membership, declining funds, and diminished authority. Even in their strongholds in Wales and the north, the chapels were in steady retreat. Not least, the challenges to Puritanism and Sabbatarianism that the war had produced severely undermined what sanctions the chapels could muster. The Church of England, too, maintained its established, national role with much difficulty after the war. Archbishops such as Randall Davidson and Cosmo Lang spoke in terms of the old cohesion and disciplines, but their message appeared increasingly ineffective.

In a formal sense, Britain was still a recognizably Christian country. Its Church leaders were still honoured and respected, indissolubly bound to Crown and landed aristocracy. Sunday was still a day of tranquillity and gloom when the trains did not run, and shops and theatres were closed, as also were public houses in Wales and Scotland. The revision of the Anglican Prayer Book in 1927–8 produced furious public debate; the old battles between Anglo-Catholic and evangelical wings of the established Church were vigorously resumed. The identification of religion with middle-class values, with the family, the community, and a safe form of patriotism, was still maintained, as the religious output of the new BBC was to indicate. So, too, was the link of religion with the empire, notably through youth movements such as the Boy Scouts and the Church Brigade. The war itself encouraged a kind of secular religiosity, symbolized in the Cenotaph erected by Lutyens in Whitehall as a memorial to the war dead and in the annual ritual of Remembrance Sunday. And yet, for all the formal trappings to remind the people of their religious inheritance through the centuries, the impact and mystique of Christianity were clearly on the wane, especially among the post-war generation and ex-servicemen.

The General Strike

The inability of the churches significantly to influence the course of events was dramatically shown during the 1926 General Strike. In that year, the terrible cycle of industrial decline, unemployment, and social bitterness led to the worst explosion of class conflict that Britain had yet known. The great strikes of 1919–21 had now passed away. The prime minister, Baldwin, called for 'Peace in our time, O Lord'. But in the greatest industry in the land, coal-mining, tension remained high, with a background of wage cuts, dismissals, and falling living standards for mining families. In April 1926 the government refused to renew a subsidy to the mining industry. On 2 May Baldwin broke off negotiations with the Trades Union Congress (TUC) delegation. Almost by accident, the unions lurched into a General Strike. For nine days (3–12 May) Britain was at a virtual standstill. Never before had the potential economic strength of the unions in challenging the government and the constitutional order been shown with more powerful effect. The Church leaders, with their call for conciliation, were impotent in the wings.

In practice, the General Strike was peaceful enough. There was no violence directed against the many blacklegs (Including many Oxford and Cambridge students who forsook their studies for the purpose) who drove buses and engaged in other strike-breaking activities. There was no violence either from, or directed against, the police or the armed forces. In the end the TUC suddenly called the strike off on 12 May, with industrial areas in Yorkshire, Cumbria, Tyneside, south Wales, and Scotland as solid as ever, and with several groups of key workers (such as power engineers) never called out at all. It was a complete defeat for the unions, and especially for the miners, who remained out on strike for several more bitter months. Britain's class war had been a brief, bloodless skirmish. For middle-class bystanders, it had even been painless, and almost great fun.

Still, it is obvious that the divisiveness revealed and reinforced by the General Strike was one powerful factor that survived to plague the unity of the nation over the next twenty years or more. In Britain's coalfields, memories of 1926, its triumphs and betrayals, were still a living reality as late as the national miners' strike of 1984–5. The General Strike may have been shown to be ineffective in the circumstances of 1926, with the unions half-hearted and the government well prepared and (in the case of such ministers as Churchill, the chancellor) even belligerent. Nevertheless, 1926 – 'Year One' in the later recollection of one Welsh miner – did demonstrate the extraordinary loyalty and class solidarity within the working-class communities of Britain, not only in older mining, steel, and shipbuilding areas but also among the newer service workers of a 'semi-skilled' category in road or rail transport and distribution. The class divisions of the country were starkly revealed, even if they did not spill over into physical violence. A deep suspicion also was displayed about the alleged neutrality of the police or the civil service, even perhaps of the newly formed BBC, which had in fact fought hard to preserve its independence in the face of governmental pressure. In mining districts, the General Strike brought a legacy of victimization by mine-owners, swingeing wage cuts, and attempts to undermine the basic role of the Miners' Federation as the voice of the workers. If demagogic miners' leaders such as Arthur Cook moved on to the sidelines, their successors in the unions and the Labour Party were no more accommodating towards a social system so manifestly distorted in its rewards and opportunities, and which made such a mockery of the supposed social unity of the war years. As Britain continued to limp through the depression years, memories of the General Strike endured, and a heritage of class protest along with it.

Social Division

In the later twenties, the land settled down into a pattern that endured until the 1940s. The population continued to grow, if more slowly; it rose from 40,831,000 in 1911 to 42,769,000 in 1921, and to 44,795,000 by the 1931 Census. But within it there were deep and growing contrasts, as younger writers such as George Orwell were later to emphasize. For much of southern England and the Midlands, the twenties were a time of growing contentment and prosperity. There were many housing developments in the form of suburban middle-class estates, stemming from the abortive Addison housing programme of 1919–21 and later schemes by Neville Chamberlain which gave a direct subsidy to private house-builders. A larger proportion of the population emerged from the war with middle-class aspirations – home ownership; a quiet family environment; more leisure pursuits (there were, for instance, over a million cars in private hands by 1930 of which the most celebrated was the 'Baby' Austin); and domestic comforts and mechanical aids such as Hoovers. The power of broadcasting through the BBC brought entertainment and instruction into the privacy of the home. For the junior managers, civil servants, school teachers, skilled workers, and others, members of the white-collar administrative and professional groups that had expanded so dramatically between 1880 and 1918, the twenties were not such a bad time, with prices starting to fall, houses more freely available on easy terms, and more leisure interests to pursue. Newer, technologically-advanced industries were mushrooming, notably the modern car plants of Herbert Austin at Longbridge in the Midlands and William Morris at Cowley, near Oxford. New patterns of suburban residential life flourished around them. For such people, the humdrum, reassuring values symbolized by the nature-loving prime minister, Baldwin, embodying in his own person the

4. Mass production at Morris Motors, Cowley, Oxford, 1929. Here the body foundation is being rubbed down after the first coat of paint. The car industry, pioneered by William Morris at Cowley and Herbert Austin at Longbridge, made a dramatic impact on British economic life and leisure patterns in the twenties

message of 'safety first', seemed attractive after all the unwanted excitements of the war and the General Strike.

Yet for many other areas, it was a time of growing despair and disillusion. The countryside, for instance, was sunk in depression in the twenties after the brief, heady revival of the war years. The rural population steadily declined, especially in the more mechanized agricultural sector of the wheat-growing areas of southern England. Prices of farm products fell; the level of rural incomes declined; the vitality of small country towns, from the Highlands to Cornwall, became impoverished. British country life preserved its traditional unchanging appearance on the surface; the 'green revolution' vastly enlarged the number of small landowners in the 1918–26 period, the greatest transformation in landholding since the Norman Conquest. But beneath

27

the surface was a pattern of indebtedness, burdens of mortgages and bank loans, and visible decay which saw the gap in the quality of life between town and country growing wider. Since much of British literature took the countryside as its basic point of reference, this potentially had serious cultural, as well as social, implications.

In the older industrial communities, especially in the north and north-east of England, industrial south Wales, and the Clydeside belt of mid-Scotland, and in the slums of Belfast across the Irish Sea, it was a time of mounting despair. The inadequacy and squalor of working-class housing and living conditions became increasingly well documented in the twenties, as did the environmental decay that cast a pall over older areas such as Jarrow, Wigan, or Merthyr Tydfil. Along with damp, insanitary housing and poor schools and public services went appalling figures of child illness and mortality, tuberculosis for the middle-aged, lung disease for miners, and physical deformity for the old. There was a markedly lower life expectancy in the older industrial regions of the north, Wales, and Scotland, than in the county towns and spas of the English south-east and the West Midlands. The social gulf grew ever wider in the twenties, made more severe still by the endless unemployment which afflicted older industries such as steel-making, shipbuilding, and coal-mining, all of them starved of capital investment. The decision to return to the gold standard at the pre-war parity in 1925 was one taken by Churchill as chancellor, in the face of biting criticism (after the event) from Keynes but with the broad endorsement of most orthodox economists and business people. It meant a serious overvaluing of British coal and steel exports, and a still higher rate of unemployment for the workers producing them. In terms of the quality of educational and medical facilities, of amenities such as libraries, swimming baths, or public parks, the social divisions were ever more apparent in the land over which Baldwin serenely presided. The era of 'safety first', with all its secularization, meant (according to some famous lectures by the socialist economic historian R. H. Tawney, published in 1929) the establishment of a new 'religion of inequality'.

Among its features, two-thirds of the aggregate national wealth was owned by 400,000 people (less than 1 per cent of the population), along with immense disparities in the quality of life throughout British society.

Traditional Order

Yet this growing social division occasioned surprisingly little revolt or protest at the time. In part, this was because of the warm solidarity of the working-class world which generated its own values, culture, and entertainment, even during the depression years. The relics of that period – the working-men's clubs and libraries; the vibrant world of the miners' lodge, the choir, and the brass band; the credit base provided by the 'Co-op' in working-class communities – may now seem remote even from soap operas such as *Coronation Street*. But they do testify to the strength and optimism of working-class life even in those gloomy years. The anodyne of mass entertainment was also encouraged by the rulers of the people to help promote patriotic loyalty. This 'bread and circuses' tradition dated from the Victorian music-hall. Many of its heroes such as George Robey (who had refused a knighthood) still flourished. But it was an art form rapidly being outstripped by the new silent and talking pictures: Charlie Chaplin and Mary Pickford were now the darlings of the halls. Beyond the innate resilience and dignity of working-class Britain, there were still qualities that kept the land relatively peaceful and integrated. These may have owed something to the much-maligned governments of the time. Chamberlain's active and creative period as minister of health (1924–9), which effectively saw the end of the old Poor Law, was one notable milestone in this process. The football crowds of the cloth-capped workers and the aspiring life-styles of the new middle class in the suburban housing developments were bound together by some semblance of common patriotic values. Familiar symbols could unite them all – perhaps the ever-popular figure of George V, perhaps the passive reassurance offered by Baldwin. The 1925 Empire Exhibition at the new Wembley Stadium was an occasion for much national pride. The sporting hero of the decade was Jack Hobbs, opening batsman for Surrey and England, who in 1925 overtook the record number of centuries (125) scored by the legendary W. G. Grace. Modest, unprotesting, a devoted church-goer and teetotaller, and a model family man, Jack Hobbs was the prototype of the loyal artisan dedicated to Crown and country. He was a professional 'player' content to be led by amateur public-school 'gentlemen' (who entered the Lord's playing arena by a different gate). He always played a straight bat and always accepted the umpire's verdict, however disappointing or mistaken, without complaint. Jack Hobbs's placid, kindly personality provided an acceptable touchstone for a society struggling to preserve a traditional order in the swirling tides of the post-war transformation.

Chapter 3
The Thirties

The twenties ended in a confused haze of nostalgia and innovation. The pomp and affluence of 'high society' and court life were as resplendent as ever. Cigarette cards and magazines acclaimed the personal appeal of social celebrities such as the aged tea magnate 'Tommy' Lipton or hostesses such as Lady Londonderry. Familiar giants still bestrode the land elsewhere. Elgar survived as Master of the King's Musick until 1934; Kipling remained actively writing until 1936; Hardy died, full of years and honour, in 1928. The mood of 'safety first' permitted only the most guarded forms of innovation. Its political figurehead in the later twenties was the Labour leader, MacDonald, called upon to form a second Labour government in 1929. MacDonald had a background of anti-war protest in 1914–18, but as a reassuring figure in the General Strike, the hammer of socialist extremists, and intimate of salons in high society, he seemed to be comfortingly locked within the aristocratic embrace. A licensed rebel, he was a safe enough symbol for a society committed to modest, but controlled, change. With Lloyd George now an isolated veteran and Churchill actively excluding himself from the Tory mainstream because of his die-hard views on Indian self-government, MacDonald appeared to be a reliable guide in taking a few measured steps towards the apocalypse.

The Second Labour Government

In fact, the second Labour government proved to be a disaster. In large part, this was because of forces far removed from political control. The crash in the American Stock Exchange in October 1929, followed by a downward spiral of trade and employment, was beyond the reach of any government to correct. For all that, it was all too apparent that the British Labour government had little to offer as a socialist or any other kind of palliative to unemployment that rose with alarming rapidity to reach nearly 3 million of the insured population at its peak in late 1932. Although unemployment gradually declined later in the thirties, in fact industrial stagnation and social decay continued. Beyond the world-wide forces of overproduction and a slump in demand, there were factors peculiar to Britain alone. There was here an industrial structure unduly geared to a declining range of traditional industries: coal, steel, textiles, and shipbuilding. There was a history of low investment, overmanning, and inefficient work practices, intensified by a culture that for decades had elevated humane disciplines and gentlemanly virtues in place of business education or entrepreneurial skills. The entire industrial and manufacturing base contracted with extreme violence. There was no sign of recovery visible until 1935. Long before then, the spectacle of hopelessness and despair in mining and other areas, of hunger marches and demonstrations by the unemployed, of the rigours of 'life on the dole' with all the helplessness and hopelessness that were implied had become one to which the great British public had become resigned or immune.

There were those who argued that a new kind of political initiative was required to regenerate and revitalize the nation and its economy, and to propel them in new directions. In the left centre, Lloyd George remained throughout the thirties an ageing, largely disregarded prophet, urging the need for a New Deal on the American model. On the far left, there was a variety of nostrums proposed, from the collectivism of the Socialist League, and later the Left Book Club, to the pure sectarianism of the tiny Communist Party. Sidney and Beatrice Webb claimed to see the future working in Soviet Russia. On the radical right, Sir Oswald Mosley left first the Conservative, then the Labour Party, and tried to create a British variant of Fascism with an admixture of corporate planning and anti-Semitism. Meanwhile the veteran socialist writers, Shaw and H. G. Wells in their different ways promoted the cause of a planned, antiseptic, scientific utopia. But the most popular solutions were sought within the traditional mix of British politics. By August 1931 it was obvious that MacDonald's Labour government was in desperate straits. The climacteric arrived with a massive run on the pound, accompanied by the publication of the May report which alleged that high government spending and an unbalanced budget were the root causes of industrial collapse. The government was urged to cut social spending, including the social benefit which was all that the unemployed had in order to subsist at all. The Cabinet was hopelessly divided, buffeted between the bankers and the TUC. On 23 August MacDonald resigned.

The National Government

The next morning, however, instead of a Conservative–Liberal administration taking his place, it emerged that MacDonald was to stay on as prime minister of a new 'National Government' from which almost all his own Labour Party colleagues would be excluded. At a subsequent general election in October, this government (which had latterly taken Britain off the gold standard and devalued the pound) was returned with a huge majority, with 556 supporters, and the Labour Party reduced to a mere 51, with almost all its leading former ministers defeated at the polls. This National Government was to set the tone for Britain in the thirties. MacDonald, its figurehead, gradually faded from the scene, an increasingly pathetic personality. Baldwin lingered on until 1937. He was still able to summon up immense reserves of political and tactical skill, as when he pushed through a bill to grant more self-government to India in 1935, or in his total outmanoeuvring of Edward

VIII in 1936 when that uncrowned monarch flouted popular convention by seeking in vain to retain his crown and also to marry a divorced American woman, Wallis Simpson. But the main energy within the government came from a new technocratic style of Conservative, freed from the rural stereotypes of Victorian days. Dominant among them was Chamberlain, heir to a famous Birmingham dynasty, the outstanding figure in political life in the thirties, at home and (later) abroad. Chamberlain it was who led a half-recovery of the economy in the earlier part of the decade, with much investment in housing and in consumer durables, and new affluence for advanced industrial zones of the East Midlands and southern England. Emigration from older regions such as south Wales, Durham, Cumberland, and Scotland was balanced by new growth in the suburbs and the centres of light industry. There was a distinctive, managerial, regulatory style in government, Britain's 'middle way' in economic policy. There were benefits for farmers in the form of milk and other marketing schemes and production quotas, and advantages for urban and suburban residents such as improved transportation (the London 'tube' being a notable example), extended gas and electricity services, and cheap housing. A century of free trade was buried at the Ottawa Conference in 1932 when a new commercial system of tariffs and imperial preference, due to last until the 1970s, was inaugurated. The effect of tariffs upon the British economy was deeply controversial, but the cartelized steel industry was one industrial giant that appeared to show some benefit. The voters were duly grateful. They returned the National Government – now almost wholly Conservative – with a comfortable majority in the 1935 general election, and gave Chamberlainite managerial Conservatism a broad support until new divisions emerged over foreign policy at the end of the decade.

Class and Regional Division

The politics of the National Government were based, unequivocally and unapologetically, on class and regional division. The older industrial areas were placed under the aegis of the 'special areas' schemes. In popular parlance, industrial Scotland, the north-east, Cumbria, much of Yorkshire and Lancashire, and South Wales were the 'depressed areas', self-contained societies only visible to the outside world when their refugees appeared in London and Birmingham to take part in hunger marches or to beg for coppers from theatre queues. There was an ironic, self-sustaining pattern about life in these so-called 'depressed' communities. There, industry was contracting, which meant that their rateable income fell further; this meant that amenities decayed still more, industrial decline was accelerated, and the entire, repetitive cycle became ever more severe.

Some of the most powerful literature of the time – George Orwell's somewhat ambiguous saga of *The Road to Wigan Pier*, Walter Greenwood's pathetic account of *Love on the Dole*, Lewis Jones's moving treatment of life in Welsh mining villages in *Cwmardy* and *We Live* – evokes poignantly the consequences of this structural poverty upon the social and cultural sensibilities of the time. But little was done to remedy the causes. There were local philanthropic gestures by the Quakers and other idealists. There was some assistance from the government through the special areas commissions, although virtually nothing was done to diversify or overhaul the industrial base of these areas by a new regional policy. Thomas Jones ironically proposed that they might be turned into open-air archaeological museums, while trains carried off their inhabitants to the delights of employment at Dagenham or Hounslow. There were also novelties such as trading estates which offered inducements to industrialists to group together and move into older industrial areas by offering cheap rates or investment grants. The town of Slough in Buckinghamshire, for instance, became a focus for much industrial activity in the thirties – while its architectural horrors became the target for the unwontedly bitter satire of John Betjeman. But, in general, a combination of the constraints imposed by the Treasury and the Bank of England, and a lack of urgency by government, kept the areas of staple industry effectively without support. Not until the impact of rearmament in the period that followed the 1935 Defence White Paper, with its emphasis on engineering and aircraft production, was there a significant rise in employment.

But the main reason why so little stimulus was provided for the industrial regions crucified by depression was that they were self-contained and limited in extent. The majority of the population in other parts of Britain found that life after the holocaust was acceptable and in many ways agreeable. The thirties were a time of very low inflation, cheap private housing, and a growing choice for consumers. An average of 345,000 houses was built annually between 1933 and 1937. The motor car industries and electrical, chemical, and textile concerns continued to thrive. In the Midlands, towns like Leicester and Coventry experienced unprecedented growth and affluence. The rewards of life were ever more apparent. Professional footballers for Herbert Chapman's Arsenal, though poorly paid, enjoyed a diet which included steak and champagne. In outer London, the spread of the 'tube', north towards Cockfosters on the edge of Hertfordshire, or west towards Uxbridge on the borders of Buckinghamshire, illustrated the expansion of the service and professional sectors of the white-collar population. In growing suburban communities such as Hendon, Harrow, or Kingsbury, there were smart shopping precincts, many new cinemas, and football grounds. The untidy ribbon of semi-detached middle-class housing stretched far along arterial roads and bit deep into the surrounding countryside, relatively unhampered by environmental controls designed to preserve the 'green belts' around cities. The Western Avenue out of London became a byword for uncontrolled industrial and residential development, with a miscellany of factories in debased historicist styles (which a later generation, incongruously enough, often regarded as monuments of modern art). If one explanation for the lack of social change in Britain amidst the unemployment and depression of the thirties lies in the lack of political and economic power vested in the older industrial areas, another lies in the growing commitment to a pleasing and acceptable form of suburban life by larger and larger sections of the population left relatively unscathed by the bleak years.

Britain in the thirties, then, displayed a surprising degree of stability in a European continent which saw totalitarianism engulf Germany, Italy, and Austria, and the French and Spanish republics cast into disarray. The social and cultural hierarchy changed very little. The prestige of Parliament, of the law courts, and of a highly stratified educational system, headed by Oxford and Cambridge, that remained almost totally a public-school preserve all remained as high as ever. The monarchy retained its esteem by responding subtly to marginal changes in the outlook of the mass democracy: George V's attendance at the annual working-class festival of the Wembley Cup Final was one instance. The king's silver jubilee in 1935 provoked widespread national rejoicing. Even the brief crisis associated with the abdication of Edward VIII left the monarchy as an institution essentially unimpaired. The nation remained comfortably isolated from a strife-torn Continent, inhabited by faraway peoples of whom the British knew little.

The Arts

In the arts, the thirties were in many ways a remarkably flourishing and creative period. In poetry, the most important figure remained Eliot, a conservative Anglo-Catholic of American birth, whose 'Four Quartets' appeared from 1930 onwards and notably during the war. Eliot, in fact, increasingly found the drama a more congenial art form, starting with *Murder in the Cathedral* (1935), a powerful commentary on the martyrdom of Thomas Becket. The most influential writers of the period, however, reacted strongly against what appeared to them to be the withdrawal and detachment of the Bloomsbury ethos in the twenties. In the maelstrom of the time, younger poets such as W. H. Auden, Stephen Spender, Cecil Day-Lewis, and Louis MacNeice reflected the political excitements of the time. Auden's celebrated poem 'Spain' (1937), inspired by his brief period of service in the Civil War, epitomized the current literary mood. It is significant that all these young poets flirted with a kind of neo-Marxism, if they did not actually become Communists. Conversely, two of the abler young novelists of the time, Evelyn Waugh and Graham Greene, were converts to Roman Catholicism, albeit with very different political and other outlooks.

British music was less volatile. Elgar, Master of the King's Musick, died in 1934, but he had written little since his melancholy, autumnal cello concerto in 1919. The romantic strains of Gustav Holst and Frederick Delius had to contend with the experimental endeavours, atonal, even unstructural, of the followers of Igor Stravinsky and Arnold Schoenberg. The tone poems of Arnold Bax and Ralph Vaughan Williams, a contemporary enough figure in his diatonic compositional techniques, yet deeply English in his reliance on traditional airs and themes, demonstrated how modernity could be safely reconciled with the native musical tradition.

In the visual arts, the thirties was a period of great excitement and innovation, both in sculpture and in painting. A new vitality for British sculpture was heralded by the work of Henry Moore, son of a Yorkshire miner, and the disciple of Jacob Epstein; another pioneer was Barbara Hepworth, the wife of the painter Ben Nicholson. British painting was also unusually vigorous at this period, ranging from the rustic Christian symbolism of Stanley Spencer to Nash's successful engagements with French surrealism. Britain was generally a better country to look at in the thirties, with much-needed innovation in architecture and design, without precedent since the heyday of Norman Shaw, Charles Voysey, and Charles Rennie Mackintosh before 1914. From dramatic set-piece public buildings which manifested the influence of Walter Gropius and the German Bauhaus, through industrial factories and Odeon cinemas with art nouveau or art deco overtones, down to mundane but important landmarks such as Frank Pick and Charles Holden's attractive new underground railway stations for London Transport, British architecture offered many departures and a real sense of liberation. At a more accessible level, the new life shown by the Royal Academy and by such accepted popular arts festivals as Sir Henry Wood's London 'proms' at the Royal Albert Hall suggested some qualified cultural advance, if hardly a cultural revolution.

Foreign Affairs

In a variety of ways, then, Britain in the thirties showed distinct signs, outside the older industrial areas, of being a land at peace with itself, and enlivened by some cultural imagination. But the mood began to change abruptly in 1937, not through any immediate domestic disunity or reappraisal, but through the external impact of foreign affairs. Much of Britain's internal harmony in the twenties and thirties had been founded on a quiescent foreign policy. The mood dictated by Keynes in 1919, the mood that had dislodged Lloyd George in 1922, had permeated the whole society. Right-wing reluctance to engage in overseas military adventures was countered by a profound belief on the left that the 1919 peace settlement was in any case vindictive and morally indefensible, the product of national and imperial rivalries rather than of a yearning for a more harmonious world. In the twenties, Britain's defences were gradually run down, with little public protest, based on the 'ten year' premiss that no major war would be fought within the next decade. The battle fleet was especially cut back in this period, most enthusiastically by Churchill himself while at the Treasury. The giant new naval base at Singapore, recently completed, already seemed an anachronism. The main military commitment was to the Raj in India, but a gradual, partial accommodation with Mahatma Gandhi and the Congress movement enabled the British garrison in the subcontinent to be reduced slowly from 57,000 in 1925 to 51,000 in 1938. Equally, the increasingly harmonious relations with the Irish Free State, culminating in the 'agreements' of 1936 and the virtual wiping out of all debts owed to Britain by Ireland minimized another potential source of military or naval difficulty.

The public mood in the early thirties remained a passive one, even after the advent of Adolf Hitler as chancellor in Germany in January 1933. The British labour movement was pacifist-inclined, with a few exceptions such as Ernest Bevin of the Transport and General Workers. It opposed voting arms estimates on behalf of a right-wing National Government. On the socialist left, there were advocates of a Popular Front such as Sir Stafford Cripps, who urged the need for an alliance with the Soviet Union and argued that socialism alone was the true remedy for international discord. Conversely, most Conservatives had no wish for an adventurous foreign policy, especially since Baldwin had assured the people that there was no real defence possible in a future war which would be determined largely by air power. The bomber would always get through. There was scant Conservative enthusiasm for upholding the authority of the League of Nations in crises in Manchuria in 1931 or Abyssinia in 1935. There were those on the right, notably some press lords, who declared that there was common ground between Great Britain and Hitler's Germany, bound together by Teutonic racial origins and anti-Communism. A miscellaneous group of politicians and journalists found a haven in Lord and Lady Astor's mansion at Cliveden, by the Thames, near Marlow. It was widely believed to be turning the mind of the Foreign Office in these fellow-travelling directions.

When the opportunity for action came, public opinion was resistant. Hitler marched into the Rhineland in early 1936, in direct contravention of the Versailles settlement. But only a few voices, like the isolated and unpopular Churchill, called for a military response from Great Britain. Earlier, the British public had generally endorsed, though with much embarrassment, the appeasement policy of the Foreign Office following the Italian invasion of Abyssinia. In effect, the Italians were allowed to occupy this ancient empire in the Horn of Africa with the minimum of British involvement, economic or military. Formal commitments were made to the League and to the spirit of collective security, but they added up to little enough. Sir Samuel Hoare, the foreign secretary, was offered up as a public sacrifice during the Abyssinian crisis, but it was clear that the appeasement of Benito Mussolini's Italy was a collective government decision. Cabinet records now available confirm the point. In any event, Hoare re-entered the government a few months later with little controversy. Again, in Spain where a left-wing, democratically elected Republican government was subjected to invasion by a right-wing Nationalist force led by General Franco, with later armed assistance from Italy and Germany, the British government adhered rigidly to 'non-intervention', even if this meant the eventual downfall of democracy in Spain. The advent of the powerful figure of Chamberlain in October 1937, a confident man committed to an active, positive pursuit of a working accommodation with the Fascist dictators, as opposed to Baldwin's passive style of appeasement, confirmed a growing mood of non-involvement in Europe. Key figures in the civil service such as Sir Horace Wilson and Sir Nevile Henderson (ambassador to Berlin) pushed this policy forward.

Change in the Public Mood

At various levels, however, the public mood suddenly began to change. Even the government began to turn its mind to the need to overhaul the national defences, especially in the air. From 1935 onwards, a new fighter-based air force was in the making, backed up by the latest technology invested in 'radar' and other anti-aircraft and defence systems. Through men like Henry Tizard and his rival Frederick Lindemann, the voice of scientific innovation was again sporadically heard in the corridors of power. By 1937 the rearmament programme was visibly under way, despite pressure from the Treasury, which voiced concern at the effect on the balance of payments. Privately, it is now known that a wider range of financial relationships was entered into with the United States which alone could underwrite the arms programme capable of being launched by a Britain still in economic difficulties. More widely, the public psychology was deeply stirred by events in the Spanish Civil War. Not only poets such as Auden or prose writers like Orwell, but many scores of British working-class volunteers who fought with the International Brigade, were being propelled towards a new commitment to internationalism. Jewish refugees from Germany brought the reality of Hitler's regime and of anti-Semitism home to British opinion. Even on the Labour left, trade union leaders such as Bevin and Walter Citrine turned vigorously against neo-pacifist Labour politicians who denied armed assistance to trade union and labour groups crushed in Fascist Germany and Austria. Chamberlain's equilibrism was harder to sustain, especially for a prime minister so lacking in the skills of flexibility.

The German advance in 1938, the seizure of Austria, and the subsequent threat to Czechoslovakia, ostensibly on behalf of the Sudeten Germans in the western fringe of Bohemia, produced a national crisis of conscience. Chamberlain responded with managerial decisiveness. At Berchtesgaden, Bad Godesberg, and finally at Munich in September 1938, he came to terms with Hitler. In effect, he allowed the Germans to annex Sudetenland on the basis of any timetable they chose, without British or French armed retaliation. For a brief moment, it seemed that this policy of surrender had mirrored the public's response. Chamberlain returned in triumph, announcing, in an ominous phrase, that it was to be peace in our time. But this abdication of responsibility could no longer adequately be justified. Those who have claimed that Chamberlain was seeking a breathing space, in order for Britain to challenge Germany more effectively in military terms later on, do not find support from the records of Cabinet deliberations. The criticisms of Churchill and his associates, and even of Eden, who had recently resigned from the Foreign Office in protest at Chamberlain's conduct of foreign affairs, now accorded far more precisely with popular sentiment. By the end of 1938, as it became clear that Munich had really meant the sacrifice of Czechoslovak democracy to armed aggression, nationwide anger was overwhelming. Chamberlain, so impregnable a figure a few months earlier, the most powerful prime minister since Lloyd George in 1916, suddenly looked like a man on the run. Rearmament was stepped up and new negotiations begun with the engineering trade unions to try to build up munitions and aircraft production.

When Hitler finally invaded Prague in March 1939, public anger exploded. Chamberlain was forced by outside pressure to enter into a military commitment to defend Poland, a land in Eastern Europe far away from British shores, with no guarantee that the Soviet Union would assist in protection of Poland's eastern frontiers. A century of almost unbroken British non-involvement in continental Europe, dating from the winding up of the Peninsular War in 1812, was abruptly reversed. The government was stampeded by a horrified public opinion. There was even a formal attempt to conclude an alliance with the Soviet Union, although things went so slowly that in the end Russia formed a pact with Germany instead in August. During the summer, there was evident a new mood of determination to resist German aggression with the full combined resources of the nation and the empire. On 1 September 1939 Hitler took the fateful step of invading Poland. After a few desperate attempts to patch up a last-minute compromise, Chamberlain announced in a broadcast on 3 September that Britain had declared war on Germany. There was scarcely any dissent, even from the tiny Communist Party, many of whose leading figures opposed the official Moscow line and took up the anti-Fascist cause. In the House of Commons, it was a Labour member, Arthur Greenwood, who 'spoke for England', and, as events showed, for virtually all of Wales, Scotland, Northern Ireland, and the dominions as well.

In the later stages of the appeasement controversy, the climate of public debate became unprecedentedly bitter. The complacency of the early thirties was set aside. There was the continuing hostility between the National Government and the Labour Party over the unending tragedy of unemployment, and the scandals of the 'dole' and the operation of the 'means test'. Added to this was a powerful rift on the right between the 'men of Munich', Chamberlain, Simon, Sir Samuel Hoare, and their followers, and the nationalist critics headed by Churchill, who denounced the policy of craven appeasement as dishonourable. Episodes such as the distant impact of events in Czechoslovakia brought left- and right-wing protest together, as Spain or Abyssinia could never have done. Domestic and international conflicts merged into one passionate, turbulent whole. Chamberlain, the architect of much of the prosperity of the thirties, the titan of the suburban middle class, the dominant leader of the decade, suddenly became the hated symbol of a fraudulent, decadent political order. He became foremost among the 'guilty men' so brilliantly denounced by two young radical journalists, Michael Foot and Frank Owen, in a fierce polemic in 1940, perhaps the greatest feat of political pamphleteering since the days of John Wilkes.

Any society presided over by Chamberlain at such a time should have found it hard to unite behind a common cause. Yet, as in August 1914, Britain did so. Indeed, when war broke out in 1939 there was a unanimity that pervaded all regions and classes. As in 1914, the war was represented publicly as a crusade on behalf of oppressed nationalities and persecuted races – which, indeed, it largely was, and far more plausibly so than in 1914. Middle and working class, capitalist and worker, socialist and conservative entered the war for different motives, or perhaps with different priorities along the political spectrum. But broad imperatives survived to create a new consensus. As 20 years earlier, Britain regained its sense of unity and national purpose amidst the challenge and turmoil of total war.

Chapter 4
The Second World War

The public mood after the outbreak of the Second World War was notably less passionate or strident than after August 1914. Neither the militarism nor the pacifism of that earlier conflict was echoed now. In large measure, this was because of the curious features of the early months of the war. During the so-called 'phoney war' period down to April 1940, the fighting seemed remote, almost academic. It is a curious, twilight phase well portrayed in Evelyn Waugh's novel *Put out More Flags*. There were massive air-raid precautions, trenches in public parks, barrage balloons aloft, and anti-aircraft weaponry deployed on public buildings. Thirty-eight million gas masks were distributed to men, women, and children; hundreds of thousands of schoolchildren were evacuated from major cities to distant, and presumably safer, rural areas (though many later drifted back home). Rationing of food, clothing, petrol, and other commodities suddenly became commonplace. The war itself was at first uneventful, with traditional pleasures such as the long-range enjoyment of a British naval victory, when the German battleship *Graf Spee* was fatally cornered by three smaller British vessels in the estuary of the river Plate off Montevideo harbour in late 1939.

The uncertainty of the public mood was mirrored by the ambiguous nature of the government. Although the Cabinet had been reconstructed, to include Churchill himself, back at the Admiralty as in

5. Children in the war. Evacuees arriving at Eastbourne, Sussex, at the outbreak of war in 1939 (*top*). In all, 827,000 schoolchildren were evacuated from major cities to seaside towns and rural areas in the autumn of 1939 to escape from German bombing raids, though many later returned home. Gas masks were distributed to children at school (*bottom*) in case the Germans used gas. In fact, the masks proved to be quite unnecessary

1914, it was still the regime of the old gang, the National Government of 1931 writ large. The trade unions in particular looked with deep suspicion at an administration still headed by their old adversary and class enemy, Chamberlain. Then in April 1940 the cold war hotted up. The Germans invaded Norway, scattering before them the British naval and military forces at Narvik. Soon afterwards, the Netherlands and Belgium were overrun, and the French army broke up in disorderly retreat. The security of the British Isles themselves was now under clear and pressing threat.

The old regime of the thirties could survive no longer. In a fateful division in the Commons on 7–8 May 1940, 80 Conservatives rebelled against the leadership of Chamberlain. Two days later he resigned, and Churchill now emerged as wartime prime minister, with Labour and Liberals both joining the government. The change of premier was generally free of the apparent conspiratorial intrigue of December 1916. Indeed, Churchill had a vastly broader base of support in press and Parliament, and distinctly more loyalty from the military, naval, and air high command, than Lloyd George had ever experienced.

Churchill embodied a traditional sense of patriotic unity as no one else amongst his contemporaries could ever do. War gave his career a new impetus and relevance. His inspiring oratory over the radio and in the Commons conjured up new reserves of national will-power in this 'finest hour' for his country. He was able to depict a humiliating military disaster in the retreat from Dunkirk as a kind of triumph for British ingenuity and determination. With France surrendering to the German forces by mid-June, British territorial security was threatened as never before since the days of Napoleon I in 1804. Truly the nation was alone.

Land, Sea, and Air

The extent to which Britain was prepared to defend itself in military and naval terms is debatable. On the home front, apart from mobilized reserves, the 'home guard' of civilians was later to be effectively parodied as a 'dad's army' of amateurs muddling through with good humour. Its military effectiveness was, perhaps fortunately, never put to the test. But the real battle lay in the air, where the reserves of Spitfire and Hurricane fighter aircraft were rapidly built up by the press lord, Beaverbrook, now the Minister of Aircraft Production. From mid-August onwards, the German *Luftwaffe* launched wave after wave of Blitz attacks, first on British airfields and aircraft factories, later in 1941 on London, Coventry, Plymouth, Liverpool, Hull, Swansea, and other ports and major cities. Almost miraculously, civilian morale and national defences stood firm against this terrifying bombardment. In the air, the 'few', the legendary pilots of the Spitfires and Hurricanes (who included many Poles, Czechs, and Canadians), took heavy toll of the *Luftwaffe* in August–October. By Christmas, the threat of imminent invasion had effectively passed, though the Blitz on London and elsewhere continued. Churchill's personal reputation soared; the united spirit of his people grew with it. Dunkirk and the battle of Britain in the air launched a thousand myths. They helped to encourage a latent isolationism and an unjustified feeling of national self-sufficiency, which led to a coolness towards Western European unity after the war. The British were aware that they alone of the belligerent Western democracies had escaped enemy occupation, as they had done consistently since 1066. For all that, the rhetoric of the 'finest hour' of 1940 captured the pride and the passion of what was felt to be a supreme moment of historic achievement.

The later course of the war on land, and more especially on sea and in the air, had a major long-term effect on the international and imperial status of Great Britain. It had begun by being a traditional European conflict to preserve national security and the balance of power in the West, to keep control of the Channel by extensive deployment of the British navy in the North Sea and in the northern Atlantic, along the western approaches. In effect, this aspect of the war reached a successful outcome by the summer of 1941, with the frustration of

German threats to invade Britain (about which Hitler was always in any case hesitant) and the beating off of the *Luftwaffe* attacks. With the operations of the British merchant navy and (from early 1941) American 'Lend-Lease' arrangements ensuring tolerable free supplies of food and raw materials for the rest of the war, there was no imminent danger to the British Isles themselves, even though sinkings by German U-boats continued apace. Churchill kept a close eye on the ports of neutralist Eire and its anti-British premier, de Valera. The further hazards of guided missile attack by V1 and V2 machines, launched from bases in Holland in the summer and autumn of 1944, while deeply alarming and the source of much damage to life and property in south-east England, did not seriously imperil the security of the nation either.

Imperial Themes

However, from late 1940, the war soon demonstrated wider, imperial themes. From being initially a conflict to preserve Western and Central Europe from the aggressive menace of German Fascism, the war rapidly turned into a broader effort to sustain the Commonwealth and empire as they had endured over the decades. The white dominions – Australia, New Zealand, Canada, and, far more hesitantly, South Africa – lent immediate support in terms of raw materials and armed naval and other assistance. In addition, the credits run up with India and Egypt in particular, the so-called 'sterling balances' which gave much trouble after the war, were vital in assisting with British payments for supplies, and in partially redressing the loss of overseas assets and the fall in 'invisible' income. The entry of the Soviet Union into the war in June 1941, and even more that of the United States in December 1941, following the Japanese assault on the US fleet at Pearl Harbor, ensured that the war would remain a world-wide one, fought in every continent and every ocean, and that the cosmic structure of the British Empire would come under acute threat.

Much British military, naval, and air-force effort was put into preserving the traditional lines of communication in the Middle East, centred on the Suez Canal, and the bases of the Persian Gulf and its hinterland, with their huge oil reserves. British forces fought with much success to put pressure on the Italians in Abyssinia and Somaliland, after Italy entered the war in August 1940. Even more endeavour went into preserving Egypt and the north African littoral. In 1941 the British forces under General Sir Archibald Wavell captured the whole of Cyrenaica and advanced towards Tripoli, but were later forced to retreat back towards Egypt. The fall of Tobruk in early 1942 led to a major political crisis at home, in which Churchill's own position appeared under threat.

The most important military engagement of later 1942 concerned the struggles of the British Eighth Army, under first General Claude Auchinleck then General Bernard Montgomery, to resist a German advance towards Cairo and Suez. However, the final breakthrough by Montgomery at El Alamein in November 1942 resulted in a successful and sustained British drive across modern Libya, through Tripoli, and into Tunisia. Here, Montgomery linked up with the American armies under General Omar Bradley, which had moved eastwards from the initial landing near Algiers. Subsequent allied campaigns, including the capture of Sicily and a prolonged drive through Italy, from the Anzio beach-head to the Alps, again had a strong concern with the imperial lines of strategic communication, and with control of the eastern Mediterranean. Those who argued that a second front should be launched in France in 1943, to relieve pressure on the Red Army in Russia, viewed this concentration in the Mediterranean with much frustration and anger. However, Churchill's Mediterranean commitment prevailed. In 1944, British forces again landed in Greece both to drive out the Germans and to beat down a native left-wing movement, ELAS.

In the Far East also, the war involved desperate efforts to shore up the empire at its base. The invasion of the Japanese through China into Indo-China and the Dutch East Indies, including the capture of all the American bases in the Philippines, led Churchill to place the Far East, with the approaches to the Indian subcontinent, even higher than the Middle East in the military priorities. There were dreadful losses. The most fateful of all involved the sinking of the battleships *Prince of Wales* and *Repulse* by Japanese bombs and torpedoes on 10 December 1941. There followed a rapid Japanese advance through Malaya and on 15 February 1942 the surrender of over 80,000 British and empire troops in Singapore. This disaster, the result of grave miscalculations by the commanding officer, General Percival, and by Churchill himself (who underestimated Japanese fighting power), was described by the prime minister in the House as 'the worst capitulation in British history'. It was a landmark in the fall of empire. Henceforth, for instance, Australia and New Zealand were to look to the USA for protection in the Pacific rather than to the imperial mother country.

However, the disasters went no further. Japanese advances into Burma were held off, with such forces as Orde Wingate's 'Chindits' gaining immense acclaim. British rule in India, threatened by disaffection by the Congress movement within the subcontinent as well as by Japanese assault from Burma, was sustained. By late 1944, the British position in eastern Asia and the Pacific, even with the loss of Malaya, Singapore, and Hong Kong, was still a powerful one, even if dependent on American land and naval assistance.

At last in June 1944, with the final invasion of France from the Normandy beach-heads by Allied forces under the command of General Dwight D. Eisenhower and Montgomery, the war again assumed a European aspect. British military tactics in this last phase have led to some controversy amongst military historians, especially the delays in pushing through northern France and the Low Countries. The airborne landing at Arnhem was a débâcle. Even so, in the end it was a rapid and triumphant campaign. It was General Montgomery who formally received the unconditional surrender of the German forces at Lüneburg Heath on 9 May 1945. Hitler himself had committed suicide a few days earlier. Japan also surrendered on 15 August after two atomic bombs had wrought huge devastation at Hiroshima and Nagasaki, killing over 110,000 people.

The Impact of the War

Throughout, the war gripped the national psychology, without raising either the doubts or the euphoric jingoism of the Great War of 1914–18. The most satisfying fact of all was that British casualties were so much lighter in the six years of the Second World War than in the four years of slogging trench warfare in 1914–18. This time a total of 270,000 servicemen were lost in six years, as well as over 60,000 civilians killed on the home front in German air raids. The campaigns had been more peripheral, more episodic, and in the end far more effectively conducted on a technical basis. Even veterans of the peace movement such as the philosopher Bertrand Russell felt that here was almost a good war. At the same time, all the vital questions surrounding Britain's external role remained unanswered. In the Middle and Far East, supreme strains had been put on the imperial system, even if Britain assumed control again of territories such as Hong Kong, Sarawak, Malaya, and Singapore in Asia, and British Somaliland in Africa. The Americans were concerned, at wartime conferences and at the Potsdam peace conference of July–August 1945, to speed up the process of decolonization. Churchill was led to observe anxiously that he had not become the king's minister, or fought a bloody war for six years, in order to achieve the dissolution of the British Empire. But already his outlook was being overtaken by events.

On the home front, the impact of total war was scarcely less momentous. As in the earlier war, there was a vast upheaval in the pattern and structure of the population, and a new juggernaut of centralization and State control to regulate social and economic life. Unlike 1914–18, however, the apparatus this time seemed to operate with far more justice – and more likelihood of the momentum being continued into the post-war world. The war clearly expressed a profound spirit of egalitarianism, of a type previously unknown in British history at any period. Orwell felt (in *The Lion and the Unicorn*) that a social revolution was taking place. The ration books, gas masks, identity cards, and other wartime controls afflicted the people equally and implied a mood of 'fair shares'. So did the communal sufferings during the Blitz. A notable impact was achieved by the 'evacuees', the schoolchildren removed from London, Birmingham, Liverpool, and other cities to take refuge in rural communities in England and Wales. For the first time, large sections of the nation got to meet, though not necessarily to know or like each other. The medical and food provision for the evacuated children of the urban slums meant a great improvement in their physical and mental well-being. For their parents, war miraculously meant that full employment was restored, after the terrible decay of the thirties. Egalitarianism also encouraged a new faith in social planning, even if the links between shop floor and pit-head and the drawing-board deliberations of London-based bureaucrats were not necessarily obvious or automatic. The result, however, was that, in the wartime mood of unity and equality of sacrifice, novel questions began to be asked about public policy. A profound conviction arose, equally amongst the armed forces, that this time the 'land fit for heroes' would not be so wantonly set aside as it was widely felt to have been in the years after 1918. This mood was captured with much precision by the wartime illustrated magazine *Picture Post*, edited by Tom Hopkinson, by the newspaper the *Daily Mirror*, and by the popular radio talks of the Yorkshire author J. B. Priestley, whose William Cobbett-like style of native radicalism achieved widespread appeal.

Social Innovation

The most celebrated document of this mood was the Beveridge report of November 1942. The work of an austere academic economist, it outlined an exciting scheme of comprehensive social security, financed from central taxation, including maternity benefits and child allowances, universal health and unemployment insurance, old age pension and death benefits. It was, in the phrase of the time, provision 'from the cradle to the grave'. An ecstatic public response gave the uncharismatic Beveridge a new celebrity as another 'People's William'; it ensured that social policy would remain high on the public agenda after the war, along with other priorities such as a free national health service. The Barlow report (actually issued in 1940) visualized a complete overhaul of the stagnant 'depressed areas'. Subsequently the 1945 Distribution of Industry Act began a long-overdue process of reversing the economic decline of areas such as north-east England and south Wales by diversifying and modernizing their economic infrastructure. The Uthwatt report of 1942 outlined a new dynamic approach to town planning, with 'green belt' provision around major conurbations, new controls over land use, and 'new towns' to cater for the overspill of older cities. Underlying all these wartime blueprints was a commitment to full employment, spelt out in the 1943 budget and a government White Paper of 1944. The tragedy of stagnation and economic and human waste that had crucified many communities in the thirties would not be repeated. Leaders of the unemployed marchers then, people such as 'Red Ellen' Wilkinson, MP for Jarrow and prominent in the 1936 Hunger March, were now active in government.

Underpinning this vogue for social innovation was the transformation of fiscal policy, with a commitment to counter-cyclical policies, a manpower budget, and the management of demand. These were taken up even by such traditionalist wartime chancellors as Kingsley Wood and Sir John Anderson. Keynes himself served at the Treasury and greatly influenced the powerful Economic Section of the Cabinet. The leading critic of the post-war settlement of 1919, he was now a key figure, not only in domestic budgetary policies, but also in external financial arrangements, including the attempt to rationalize international trade and currency through the Bretton Woods agreement. The most radical nostrums were now proposed in the most staid of circles: nationalization of major industries and the Bank of England; a levy on inherited capital; a salaried, State-directed medical

6. *Tube Shelter Perspective* by Henry Moore: one of a series of 'shelter drawings', based on Liverpool Street extension underground railway station, 1941. One symbol of common suffering during the war years was the use of tube stations as refuges during the London Blitz. By September 1940, 177,000 people were sleeping in the underground system. The incomplete extension running from Liverpool Street held about 12,000, many of whom stayed underground for weeks on end

profession. They all provoked growing arguments between Conservative and Labour Cabinet ministers, with angry sniping from the back benches by freebooters such as Emanuel Shinwell, a forthright Glasgow Jew, and Aneurin Bevan, a brilliant Welsh ex-miner. But such a flowering of social and intellectual debate, far more precisely conceived and of far wider appeal than the 'reconstruction' discussions of 1917–18, under the aegis of such a traditional wartime leader as Churchill, was indeed a sign of a new climate.

The Arts

In culture and the arts, the war gave some new life to old values. Literature, significantly enough, was not stimulated to anything like the same degree as in 1914–18; there was nothing remotely resembling the generation of 'war poets' of that earlier period. Some encouragement was given to war artists, officially sponsored to depict experiences in the Blitz and elsewhere: Moore, John Piper, and Graham Sutherland are three notable examples.

Interestingly, music was one art form given a powerful stimulus, especially through the patronage of the wartime creation of CEMA (Council for the Encouragement of Music and the Arts). Lunchtime piano concerts in London during the Blitz by Dame Myra Hess suggested a new popular enthusiasm for music. The composers' response came in powerful creations by Michael Tippett (a pacifist who produced a moving and humane work, *A Child of Our Time*) and the work of Benjamin Britten. The latter's *Peter Grimes*, first performed in June 1945, gave a remarkable new vitality to English opera, still largely derived from the light concoctions of Gilbert and Sullivan 50 years earlier. During the war also, the cinema became more recognizable as an innovative art form. Films such as *In Which We Serve* and *Brief Encounter* drew effectively upon wartime themes – separation, loss, sacrifice – to imbue a commercially inclined industry with some creative realism.

Of all the media for cultural communication, however, it was BBC radio which loomed largest in the public mind. Comedians like Tommy Handley, popular singers like Vera Lynn, and war reporters like Richard Dimbleby and Wynford Vaughan Thomas became the great mass entertainers and communicators of their time. In a world convulsed by unfamiliar social and intellectual ideas, the BBC remained a basically conservative, reassuring institution, committed to God, the king, and the family, to the continuities of life and the permanence of the national heritage. In the holocaust of six years of war, that appeared to be what the mass populace required and demanded.

Education and Social Change

It was, in any case, an increasingly aware and educated populace. British education had not undergone any major overhaul since 1918; its expansion had been cruelly cut back by the Geddes economies of 1922. Large sections of the working-class community had virtually no secondary schooling at all, while the proportion attending university or other higher education down to 1939 was extraordinarily small by international standards, and almost entirely of wealthy or middle-class background, save only in Wales. Hence the Butler Education Act of 1944, another social landmark of the war years, laid the framework of a new comprehensive secondary system for all, divided like Gaul into three parts – secondary modern, grammar, and technical. At the same time by giving new life to the grammar schools, and outlining a vast future investment in school building and equipment, the act helped ensure a far greater degree of literacy and of social and occupational mobility. In the post-war world, the age of the grammar-bred boy and girl would surely dawn, whatever doubts surrounded the standards of the 'modern' schools which the unsuccessful majority would attend.

The First World War had produced an official commitment to the restitution of traditional values and ideas, whatever the mass popular enthusiasm for social change, or even revolution, in both working-class circles and intellectual coteries. The Second World War saw far less division between aspiration and reality. Indeed, the congruence between a public commitment to change and a private administrative recognition that pre-war society was dangerously unjust and divisive was the most important legacy of the Second World War for the British people. One major aspect of this was that the trade unions were now very far from being the outsiders that they had been after 1918. The most powerful union leader of the day, Bevin of the Transport and General Workers, was the dominant government minister on the home front, after Churchill appointed him Minister of Labour in May 1940. Under his aegis, the unions worked with government in regulating working practices, in improving industrial conditions, and in the strategy of economic planning with an intimacy never before achieved. Citrine, secretary of the TUC, became virtually an ancillary member of the government.

There were indeed strikes during the war, notably among miners in Kent in 1942 and among boy apprentices on the Clyde in 1941 and in south Wales in 1942–3. But they were relatively minor events contrasted with the wider consensus that was emerging. By the end of the war in 1945, the TUC had drafted a revised list of public priorities, including the nationalization of major industries and public services, the maintenance of full employment, a welfare state on the lines of the Beveridge report, and a more egalitarian financial policy based on the wartime ethos of 'fair shares'.

Political Radicalism and Reconstruction

At all levels this feeling chimed in with a noticeable mood of political radicalism. Indeed, in the years 1940–5, Britain may be said to have moved more rapidly to the left than at any other period of its history. In government, Labour ministers of the Churchill administration loomed large on the home front. Bevin; Clement Attlee, the deputy prime minister; Herbert Morrison, the home secretary; Greenwood, Hugh

Dalton, and others became familiar and trusted figures. They were talismans of the faith that post-war reconstruction would indeed be carried into effect. So, too, were reformist Conservative ministers such as Butler, author of the Education Act. Their outlook harmonized with the new orthodoxies of the planners, many of them Liberal theoreticians such as Keynes or Beveridge, or simply apolitical technocrats.

Beyond the confines of Westminster and Whitehall, it was clear that the public was becoming more radical – at least, it should have been clear, since this was documented in Gallup polls in the newspapers, though little attention was paid by contemporaries to these unfamiliar forms of sociological evidence, of transatlantic origin. In by-elections, there were several successes for the vaguely Christian socialist Common Wealth Party. There was the widespread public enthusiasm for the Red Army, newly popular after Stalingrad and the advance towards Berlin. Even in the armed forces, so it was murmured, left-wing or novel ideas were being bandied about in current affairs groups and discussion circles. Letters home from servicemen in the western desert or the Far East voiced the angry determination for a better deal in the post-war world.

Reconstruction, then, was a far more coherent and deep-rooted concept as the war came to its close. In 1918, many of the blueprints had been poorly conceived and destined for rapid oblivion at the hands of the Treasury. This time it had been more plausibly a people's war. The ideas were more precise and had both more democratic impetus and more intellectual ballast. The outcome was revealed with dramatic effect as soon as the war ended. The Churchill coalition broke up with unexpected suddenness in May 1945, a few days after the German surrender and with hostilities still continuing in the Far East against the Japanese. To Churchill's dismay, the Labour Party's national executive, voicing the wishes of the rank and file, insisted that Labour's ministers leave the government. A general election was called for July.

The 'coupon election' of 1918 had been an unreal exercise throughout. Even if not polluted by the hysterical 'hang-the-Kaiser' jingoism to the extent that Keynes had suggested, that element was undoubtedly present. A general patriotic exaltation made the campaign of November–December 1918 a poor guide to the public mood. In June–July 1945, however, the spirit was more sober and focused more precisely on housing and health, full employment, and industrial regeneration, on post-war social imperatives rather than on external or imperial themes. In this sense, the power and prestige of Churchill, the revered war leader, were an irrelevance, even an embarrassment to the Conservative Party.

The result, to the general astonishment, was a political landslide without precedent since 1906. Labour made 203 gains and won, in all, 394 seats to the Conservatives' 210. Attlee, the prosaic, reticent leader of the Labour Party, found himself propelled into 10 Downing Street, at the head of a government elected with a massive majority. Alongside were such experienced figures as Bevin as foreign secretary, Morrison as deputy prime minister, Dalton at the Treasury, and Sir Stafford Cripps at the Board of Trade. It was a striking comment on the changed atmosphere of the war years, and no doubt a delayed verdict on the bitterness of the thirties, with its memories of Munich and Spain, Jarrow and the hunger marches. For a rare moment in its history, Britain appeared to present a spectacle of discontinuity and disjunction. It left ministers and the mass electorate at the same time exhilarated and bewildered. As James Griffiths, one new Labour minister, exclaimed in genuine bewilderment at the deluge, 'After this – what?'

Chapter 5
The Post-War World

In fact, one phase of continuity was to be followed by another. The Labour government of 1945–51, while productive of much domestic partisanship and occasional bitterness during its six years of office, launched a new kind of consensus, a social democracy based on a mixed economy and a welfare state which took Britain well enough through the difficult post-war transformations and endured in its essence for another generation or more. Not until the very different political and economic climate of the later 1970s did the Attlee-based legacy which emerged from the post-war period come to be challenged decisively. Until then, the balance between innovation and stability that the post-1945 regime introduced seemed to conform to the general will.

Public Sector and Welfare State

At one level, the Attlee government certainly brought about a remarkable programme of sustained reformist activity. Major industries and institutions were brought into public ownership-coal, railways, road transport, civil aviation, gas, electricity, cable and wireless, even the Bank of England. In all, 20 per cent of the nation's industry was taken into the 'public sector'. Remote groups of corporate private capitalists were replaced by remote boards of corporate public bureaucrats. Not until the nationalization of iron and steel in 1948–9 brought differences within the government to the surface did the main premises of public

7. The Labour Cabinet under Attlee, 23 August 1945. The front row contains (*left to right*) Lord Addison, Lord Jowitt, Sir Stafford Cripps, Arthur Greenwood, Ernest Bevin, Clement Attlee, Herbert Morrison, Hugh Dalton, A. V. Alexander, James Chuter-Ede, and Ellen Wilkinson. Labour was returned with a huge majority of more than 150

ownership, as spelt out in the 1945 Labour manifesto, come to be challenged.

There was also the great extension of publicly financed social welfare, popularly dubbed 'the welfare state'. The most spectacular and controversial feature of this was the National Health Service introduced by Bevan in 1946, and coming into effect in July 1948. The Health Service generated much debate at the time, and much resistance from doctors who viewed with alarm attempts to implement a salaried system to make them State employees, and to abolish the sale of private practices. However, the public consensus after the war was sufficiently powerful to force the bill through, and to enable free medical attention for all citizens to come into effect. Other notable measures included the national insurance system introduced in 1946, very much on the lines of Beveridge's wartime proposals; a new drive for State-subsidized 'council' houses which yielded well over a million new and temporary dwellings up to 1952; increased old age pensions; a raising of the school-leaving age; and child allowances.

These measures were by no means greeted with such unanimous acclaim at the time as is sometimes alleged. The government made many concessions to its critics. Bevan himself had to allow the retention of private practice by the medical profession, and 'pay beds' within the nationalized hospitals, a typically British compromise. In secondary education, the public schools flourished side by side with the State grammar schools. Indeed, the years of socialist rule after 1945 saw Eton and other privately endowed educational institutions never more thriving, with their charitable status protected by the Inland Revenue. Public housing schemes were whittled down by pressures to encourage homes for sale and the principle of a 'property-owning democracy'.

With all its limitations, however, the welfare State gained a broad measure of support, and was accepted as a vital attribute of the balanced, compassionate society over the next 20 years. Despite a ministerial fracas in April 1951, which led to the resignation of Aneurin Bevan and two other ministers over charges on dentures and spectacles, the underlying principles of a publicly supported, comprehensive welfare State survived largely unscathed. So, too, did the commitment to full employment and new regional policies that gave renewed life to once derelict areas such as the Welsh valleys, Durham, Cumberland, and the central industrial belt of Scotland. In the light of these benefits, trade unionists were prepared to accept wage freezes, devaluation, and disagreeable hardships. Their loyalty to their own government survived all rebuffs.

Changing Living Standards

Later legend made this era one of austerity and general gloom. So in some ways it was. From the outset, Britain faced a huge post-war debt. There were continuous shortages of raw materials and of basic food supplies, made worse by the lack of dollars which led to a severe imbalance of trade with North America. There were moments of near-panic like the run on sterling, following convertibility of the exchanges, in July 1947; the decision to impose devaluation of the pound against the dollar in September 1949; and the balance of payments difficulties during the Korean War in July–August 1951. Rationing of food, clothing, petrol, and many domestic commodities survived until 1954. Planning and controls, administered by faceless bureaucrats in Whitehall (and circumvented by 'spivs' and the 'black market'), became part of the conventional stereotypes of the time.

For all that, most working-class people, the vast majority of the population, viewed the years since 1945 as much the best that had been generally known since the late-Victorian heyday. Wages rose to 30 per cent above their 1938 level. There were higher living standards, guaranteed employment, and more satisfying environmental and educational facilities. In a world, too, where popular sport such as football and cricket, and also the cinema and the dance-hall, were readily accessible, the leisure aspects of the good life were catered for as well. Football stadiums such as Highbury, Villa Park, or Old Trafford attracted each week over 60,000 enthusiastic (and entirely peaceable) spectators.

In 1951, in its last few months in office, the Labour government launched a Festival of Britain, to commemorate the centenary of the Great Exhibition of 1851. At a time of economic shortages and much gloom in overseas affairs, it seemed to some jaundiced critics hardly the right time for a festival of national rejoicing. But the Festival proved a triumphant occasion. It led, amongst other benefits, to a dramatic cleaning-up of the derelict south bank of the Thames, focusing on Robert Matthew's superb new Festival Hall for music and other arts. It released new powers of creativity in architects, sculptors, and designers. At the same time, it suggested also some of the technological and manufacturing skills latent in the British people. Along the Thames at Battersea, the fun fair was a riot of gaiety and invention. The Festival was testimony to a people still vital and vigorous in its culture, still at peace with itself and secure in its heritage.

Political Harmony

In fact, the buoyancy implied by the Festival of Britain was more than sustained by the Conservatives after 1951. Churchill, Eden, Harold Macmillan, and Sir Alec Douglas-Home, the prime ministers during the period of unbroken Tory rule from 1951 to 1964, pursued a policy of social peace. The trade unions were generally permitted to develop their freedoms and collective bargaining powers that they had strengthened during the war. There were few major strikes, and no domestic violence, even in Northern Ireland. The welfare state was reinforced, with relatively few incursions into its provisions. Full employment remained a broad priority; indeed, it was thought to be ensured in perpetuity by the Keynesian methods of demand management symbolized in the financial creed of 'Mr Butskell' (a hybrid of the Tory Butler and the Labour leader, Hugh Gaitskell, which suggested the centrist policies of the time).

When unemployment again reared its head in 1959–60, the Conservatives were as vigorous in promoting interventionist regional policies as their Labour predecessors had been. The prime minister of this period, Harold Macmillan, was dubbed 'Supermac' by the (half-admiring) left-wing newspaper cartoonist, 'Vicky'. There was, therefore, no major departure from Attlee-style consensus between 1951 and 1964. The return of another Labour government under Harold Wilson by a narrow majority in 1964 – confirmed by a much larger majority in 1966 – suggested no great deviation from the broadly accepted political and social framework of the past twenty years.

Literature, Drama, and Music

Political harmony at home gave scope to experiment and innovation in the arts. After a barren decade in the 1940s, the fifties saw major works from many novelists of distinction, several of whom had begun writing before the war: Joyce Cary, Lawrence Durrell, Angus Wilson, and Iris Murdoch were among the most significant. British drama also experienced a renaissance it this period, from the avant-garde work of the Irishman Samuel Beckett and of Harold Pinter, to the social realism of committed figures such as John Osborne. His *Look Back in Anger* (1956), performed at the radical stronghold of the Royal Court theatre in Sloane Square, created a stir with its contemptuous rejection of social change in Britain since 1945. The ambiguous, romantic phenomenon of the 'angry young man' was born. In *The Outsider*, Colin Wilson captured the dilemma of the alienated intellectual.

Poetry also showed much vitality, notably through the Welsh poet Dylan Thomas, until he drank himself to death in New York in 1953. There was also the 'Ulster Renaissance' in Northern Ireland. Beyond the shores of Britain, British visitors to the United States noted the near-monopoly of British dramatists and actors on Broadway. The illusion was nourished that Britain, for all its acknowledged economic weakness and technical backwardness, could still, through its cultural attainments, play Greece to America's Rome.

British music was also unusually lively, with Britten in particular active both in composition and in opera, and older figures like William Walton also vigorous. What was perhaps more encouraging was that music-making showed clear signs of being a less esoteric or middle-class activity. School orchestras and amateur music groups flourished. Local festivals were springing up apace, with the one launched at Edinburgh in 1947 the most distinguished. A major factor in all this was state patronage through the Arts Council, however much controversy its presence and influence aroused.

One area where there was less evidence of advance, unfortunately, was architecture and town planning. The 'new towns' were mostly by-words for grim, Stalinist uniformity, while opportunities to rebuild older cities ravaged in the Blitz were too often cast aside, notably in Manchester, Swansea, and the City of London around St Paul's. Ugly, high-rise flats pierced the skyline. New civic buildings and universities were often severe and unattractive. 'Plate glass' was not a concept that commanded enthusiasm, and the design of major urban centres and older cathedral cities suffered accordingly.

Radio, Television, and Film

Elsewhere in the arts world, the BBC, in both radio and, to a much lesser degree, television, showed signs of being a cultural pioneer. The Third Programme became from 1946 a powerful stimulus to music and drama. Television became a nationwide phenomenon after 1950, and, with all its admitted limitations, served a useful social role in introducing the nation to itself. 'Independent' television, financed by advertising, began in 1954. The BBC was also valuable in catering for the interests of minorities, including intellectuals, speakers of Welsh, and Asian and other 'coloured' immigrants.

8. Margaret Rutherford, Stanley Holloway, and Paul Dupuis in a scene from *Passport to Pimlico* (1949), one of the most successful of the post-war Ealing Studios comedy films, produced by Michael Balcon

The cinema gradually became a medium for renewed artistic experimentation. It was fortified by the mass audiences that its low prices and informal atmosphere were able to attract, and its immediate freedom from the rival challenge of television. The most notable film events of the late 1940s were the Ealing Studios comedies, distinctive for their reinterpretation of traditional British themes with restrained humour and gentle tolerance. *Passport to Pimlico*, *Kind Hearts and Coronets*, and others of this genre were testimony to the continuities and coherence of British society. Far less interesting were endless films produced in the shadow of the British class system, which depicted the working class in the affectionate, patronizing, uncomprehending terms familiar to West-End theatre-goers over the generations. Foreigners were usually suspect or simply comic (as they were in the children's books of Enid Blyton, which poured forth at this time). Enduring symbols such as the friendly village 'bobby' were given sentimental currency in the film *The Blue Lamp* or in television serials like *Dixon of Dock Green*.

More positively, in the later fifties, some of the new tides sweeping through the French, Italian, and (to some degree) the American cinema had some real impact on Britain also. A wave of socially realistic films, often with sharp social comment to offer, suggested a shift in cultural attitudes. The popularity of *A Taste of Honey* or *Saturday Night and Sunday Morning*, with their searching penetration of working-class values and the human relationships moulded by them, implied a new depth and sensitivity in the British cinema industry. At a wider level, it suggested the security and stability of Britain at this transitional period in its history.

External Policy

The stability of the domestic scene was much assisted by the general quietude of external policy. Britain in 1945 was still a great power, one of the 'Big Three' at the international peace conferences. It demonstrated the fact by manufacturing its own atomic and hydrogen bombs. Until the cumulative effect of economic decline took its inevitable toll, this facade was preserved up to the Moscow Test-Ban Treaty of 1963. Britain had its own powerful defence systems, its own supposedly independent nuclear weaponry, its own sterling area, and its private strategic, trading, and financial ties with a mighty, if dissolving, empire. In medical, physical, and chemical science, Britain was still pre-eminent, as the international acclaim for such Nobel prizewinning pioneers as Alexander Fleming and Howard Florey, discoverers of penicillin, the British Francis Crick and his American colleague James Watson, discoverer of DNA, suggested.

The Retreat from Empire

However, Britain's international position was qualified by the gradual, but necessary, retreat from empire that the post-war period witnessed. It was a relentless process, even during the regime of such a veteran imperialist as Churchill. The granting of self-government to India, Pakistan, Burma, and Ceylon (Sri Lanka) by the Attlee government in 1947–9 was the key moment in the transfer of power. It was an unambiguous statement of Britain's military and financial inability, and above all lack of will, to retain possession of distant lands by force. The process of decolonization gained in momentum in the fifties, with territories in West and East Africa and elsewhere receiving their independence, even Kenya and Cyprus, where there were bloody engagements against native nationalist forces. In southern Africa, the eventual breakup of the Central African Federation in 1963 meant independence for Northern Rhodesia (Zambia) and Nyasaland (Malawi) also.

By the early 1960s, only a scattered handful of miscellaneous territories – British Honduras, the smaller islands in the Caribbean, the Falkland Islands, Gibraltar, Hong Kong, Aden, Fiji, and a few other outposts – were still under direct British rule. There was little enough

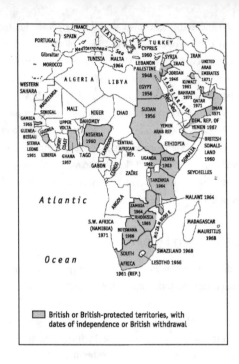

Map 1. The retreat from empire, 1947–80

nostalgic hankering for the mystique of empire now. Empire Day disappeared from the calendar of State schools; Indian civil servants anonymously returned home; the king ceased to be emperor of India.

Then in October 1956, the prime minister of the time, Eden, astonishingly engaged in covert moves with the French and the Israelis to invade the Suez Canal Zone, after the Egyptians had declared that that crucial waterway was henceforth to be nationalized. World opinion turned against Britain, even in the United States. Sterling was threatened; oil supplies dried up; the British troops withdrew ignominiously, censured by the United Nations. There were few signs of

prolonged public anger; the voices of the older imperialism were relatively muted. In the 1959 general election, the Conservatives fought, and comfortably won, on the basis of domestic prosperity – 'You've never had it so good', in the argot of Macmillan.

On the other hand, the American politician, Daniel Moynihan, could write of the new prestige of Britain in the Afro-Asian Third World for having liberated so large a proportion of the world's population without the bitterness of the French in Algeria, the Dutch in Indonesia, or the Belgians in the Congo. A world that had once listened to the liberal nostrums of Jeremy Bentham and David Ricardo, John Stuart Mill and

William Gladstone, now hearkened to the social democratic creed proclaimed by Laski and Tawney of the London School of Economics, the *New Statesman*, and (even in Opposition) the Labour Party.

In its post-imperial phase, Britain became a more introspective power, one whose role in world affairs was uncertain. As the Commonwealth connection became more ceremonial – though with important practical aspects like the operation of the sterling area and the imperial preferences for Commonwealth products such as butter and meat – the relationship with America, bittersweet in many ways, loomed ever larger. From 1949 the United States and Britain were bound together, strategically and geo-politically, in NATO. Another organization, SEATO, for South-East Asia, followed on shortly. Thereafter, British and American policies marched closely together, whether a Conservative or a Labour government was in power.

The British prided themselves on this meaning an equal 'special relationship' between the English-speaking peoples. It is clear, however, that in practice this relationship involved Britain striving desperately to maintain an illusory posture of independence. In the Korean War, in dealings with Communist China (other than its formal recognition), in the Middle East, and above all in Europe in the face of Russian threats, British and American policies were similar, if not identical. A rare attempt at rebellion such as the British involvement in the Suez operation in 1956 was quickly snuffed out. The Nassau agreements of 1962, which saw America provide Britain with its nuclear 'deterrent', the Polaris submarine, led to defence and economic dependence on the United States being more pronounced than ever.

Nearer home, there were attempts from 1947 onwards to form a political and economic union of Western Europe. From the dawn of this idea just after the war, British governments were suspicious, if not openly hostile. They cited the Commonwealth connection, the special relationship with the United States, the distinctiveness of the British constitutional and legal system, the autonomy of British socialist planning. More powerfully, most British people regarded other Western Europeans as incomprehensible aliens, with few natural ties linking them across the English Channel. The first British attempt to join the European Common Market was rebuffed by President de Gaulle of France in 1963; years passed before another effort was made. It cannot be said that the British showed any overwhelming sense of grief at this failure to be admitted to an alien institution which would mean dearer food and a threat to national sovereignty. The Euro-enthusiasts were swimming against the clear tide of public opinion.

Social Changes

In this self-contained, somewhat insular, society, the general pattern was set by consumer-led affluence. Beneath the surface, economists, the new soothsayers of the age, detected slow rates of growth and falling productivity. Sociologists unearthed deep inequalities and class divisions which prevented the modernizing of a 'stagnant society'. Attitudes to British institutions and conventions were marked by much complacency. For the British, life seemed now distinctly better. A falling birth-rate meant smaller and more affluent households. Homes were better furnished. Families increasingly had cars; they could buy their homes on cheap mortgages; they managed each summer a decent holiday abroad in Spain, France, or Italy.

Nor were these growing delights confined to the semi-detached middle class in the suburbs. Working-class people also enjoyed airlifted package holidays to the sunny Mediterranean coast, and revelled, in pubs, clubs, and elsewhere, in the freedom of choice afforded by higher wages and shorter working hours. The working-class young became a favourite target for sociological analysis and conventional head-shaking, with their more eccentric lifestyles and a more expansive pop culture. A sporting hero such as the long-haired Northern Ireland and Manchester United footballer George Best suggested very different values from those of Jack Hobbs in the twenties. The musical breakthrough effected in the early 1960s by the Beatles, a group of Liverpudlian youths, made Britain the harbinger of the supposedly 'permissive' society, in which drink and drugs were freely available, skirts spectacularly shorter, and sexual restraint much less in evidence. England's football World Cup victory in 1966 added an aura of patriotism to the new aggressiveness of the young.

In addition, middle-class reformers pioneered other social changes, assisted by the hedonistic outlook of a prime minister such as Macmillan, and the civilized tolerance of a Labour home secretary, Roy Jenkins. Sexual offences, homosexual and otherwise, were less liable to the rigours of the law. Abortion, along with the pill and other easily obtainable contraceptives, offered scope for endless sexual indulgence; there were far more divorces, and one-parent families. The youth cult seemed for a time to be sweeping the land, allegedly fostered by President Kennedy's 'New Frontier' in America. In particular, a variety of cultures mingled in British universities. Here a growing number of uprooted working-class students merged with more aggressive middle-class contemporaries to fortify the appeal to youth with the protection of mere numbers. Many new universities sprang up in the ten years after 1963, while older universities were much expanded. 'More means worse', complained some critics. Others countered that British potential was scarcely being exploited when only 5 per cent of the relevant age-group went on to higher education of any kind. Since the basic problems of subsistence were apparently being resolved by the economics of abundance, the articulate university young could turn their energies to new crusades.

The Campaign for Nuclear Disarmament in the later fifties owed much to the idealism of the middle-class young. For a time, it threatened to undermine the Labour Party as a potential party of government. Later in the sixties, the same kind of passion flowed into protest against the American war in Vietnam. Student rebellion, familiar abroad in Berkeley

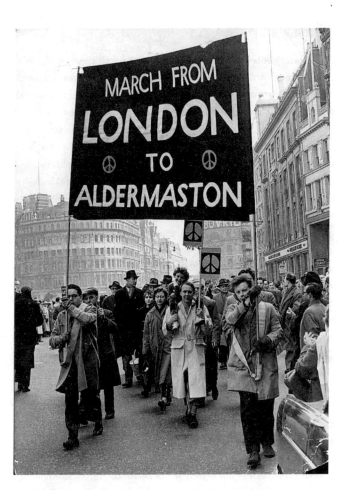

9. Aldermaston marches. The start of the first march from Trafalgar Square to Aldermaston weapons research establishment in Berkshire, 50 miles away, April 1958. This marked the beginnings of the Campaign for Nuclear Disarmament (founded February 1958), a powerful movement advocating the unilateral abandonment of nuclear weapons by Britain

or the Sorbonne, briefly flared up in British campuses, and then, equally mysteriously, petered out.

Nationalism and Racism

These movements had wider implications. Beneath the veneer of public contentment, there were in reality a variety of divisive forces that were deeply entrenched. A wide range of different groups were, in the period of Wilson's first premiership (1964–70), exploding into revolt. The young were finding the values of consumerism and conformism unappealing in a world whose ecology was being disturbed and whose very existence was threatened by weapons of unimaginable horror. Elsewhere, young people in Wales and Scotland generated a tide of nationalist protest, more familiar in the Basque regions of Spain or in French Quebec. Wales and Scotland had not fully enjoyed the economic growth of the 1950s. Their national aspirations were hardly fulfilled by such formal institutions as the secretaries of State created for Scotland and much later (in 1964) for Wales. Scottish nationalists complained, with justice, that the very title of Elizabeth II was a misnomer in their country. In Wales, there was the added theme of an ancient language and culture threatened with extinction in the unequal battle against anglicized 'admass' culture. Victory for a Welsh Nationalist at Carmarthen in a by-election in 1966 was followed by renewed civil disobedience (and a few bombing attempts) on behalf of the Welsh language. A successful Unionist response was Prince Charles's investiture as prince of Wales in 1969. In Scotland, the Nationalists captured the Hamilton seat, and several local authorities; a new anti-English mood seemed to be sweeping Highlands and Lowlands alike.

Less constitutional or placid were the demands of the 'coloured' minorities, over a million of whom had migrated to Britain from India, Pakistan, West Africa, and the West Indies since 1950. In addition to dilapidated housing and racial discrimination in employment and (sometimes) at the hands of the police, there was the added hazard of racial bigotry in older urban areas. This was fanned by the inflammatory rhetoric of a maverick right-wing Cassandra, Enoch Powell. 'Rivers of blood' were forecast in British cities on the lines of the race riots of the United States.

More disturbing still, in Northern Ireland, an artificial State kept in being by the control of the Protestant majority from 1920 onwards was in disarray. A powerful civil rights movement arose on behalf of the Roman Catholic (and usually nationalist) minority. But, in practice, attempts to maintain religious and racial harmony clearly broke down. Troops were moved into Belfast and Londonderry to preserve order. An alarming wave of bombing attacks in English cities signified that the IRA and Sinn Fein were taking the age-old struggle of Irish nationalism into a new and sinister phase. In the later sixties, with minorities on the march from Brixton to Belfast, liberal consensual Britain seemed to be breaking down, as it had almost done in 1910–14.

Economic Pressures

Hitherto the social fabric had been kept intact, at least in part, because of high and advancing living standards for the population as a whole. But clear evidence mounted up in the 1960s that increasing economic pressures were adding to the new social tensions. Britain lurched in that miserable decade from one financial expedient to another, with frequent balance of payments crises and many runs on sterling. Devaluation of the pound in 1967 did not produce any lasting remedy. Inflation began to rise significantly, especially in the early 1970s when a Conservative government under Edward Heath recklessly expanded the money supply, a misguided version of Keynesianism. All the predictions of Keynesian economists were now overturned as rising inflation was accompanied by a growing toll of unemployment as well.

At first this was confined to the older industrial regions of the north-east, Scotland, and South Wales. The rise of nationalism in the last two was much associated with the closure of collieries and factories and the laying off of labour. But by 1973 it was clear that the economic problems of Britain were having far more general consequences. The nation's capacity to generate wealth, along with its share of world trade and production, were in serious, perhaps terminal, decline. Britain seemed to have replaced Turkey as the legendary 'sick man of Europe'.

In retaliation for declining living standards, the unions replied with collective industrial power. Their membership numbers were rising fast, to reach a peak of well over 13 million in 1979. Strikes mounted up, most acutely in the case of the coal mines. A national miners' strike was called in February 1972 and was wholly successful. The Heath government experienced the full extent of the miners' ability to disrupt national production and energy supplies, despite all the contraction of the coal industry since the 1950s. Another miners' strike in February 1974 saw the government call an election on the theme of: 'Who governs Britain?' The answer, unexpectedly, was a small swing to Labour, and the government duly fell. The miners again won all their demands and their former place high in the wages table.

A widening mood of protest, a reluctance to accept traditional sanctions and disciplines, institutional power from the unions thrust against a declining productive base – these formed the ominous backcloth as Britain emerged from its brief, heady acquaintance with 'affluence' to confront the unfamiliar challenges of a new international order.

Chapter 6
From the Seventies to the Nineties

In the 1970s, Britain offered a permanent, painful case for macro-economic and sociological treatment. Its economic decline continued, comparatively in relation to almost all other developed nations, and even in absolute terms compared with earlier production levels. It was much aggravated by the dramatic change in the energy situation in 1973–4, as a result of which Britain and other Western nations suffered a fourfold increase in the price of Middle East oil. This gave new impetus to Britain's own major development in this decade, the exploitation of the oil reserves in the North Sea, and of North Sea natural gas also.

With nuclear power stations and hydro-electric schemes, as well as abundant supplies of coal, Britain was in many ways far better prepared to confront these new difficulties than many of its competitors. But the huge rise in the price of oil inevitably fuelled inflation on a scale unknown since 1919. It was reinforced by trade union pressure for enormous wage increases of anything up to 30 per cent until late 1975. British inflation continued to run at a historically high level, reaching over 20 per cent for a time in 1980, before it sank in 1982–3 to a more manageable figure of less than half that amount. Thereafter, curbs on the money supply, aided by a slow-down in wage increases and a relative fall in the real price of many commodities, saw the inflation rate subside to around 4 per cent by the autumn of 1987.

With surging price rises and pressure from wage and other unit costs, unemployment re-emerged as the major domestic scourge. By 1980 it was over 2 million, a total unknown since the thirties. With government investment and the money supply curtailed, unemployment had advanced to well over 3 million by the spring of 1983. It remained at that alarming total for the next three years, even creeping up somewhat, until some renewed economic growth saw a slight fall to below 3 million in 1987. There seemed to be a deep rot at the heart of the economy, with hundreds of thousands, many of them teenagers or other young people, doomed to perhaps years on national assistance, while public welfare services were steadily curtailed.

There was evidence of decline elsewhere as well. Although the population continued to increase, from over 50 million in 1951 to over 56 million in 1961, it was noted that there was actually a fall in the period 1975–8. The birth-rate fell sharply during the recession, while a larger proportion of the population were elderly, placing strains on the social services and necessarily reliant on the wealth created by the able-bodied still in employment.

Social Disruption

The outcome was most disruptive for the social fabric. An initial period of runaway inflation in 1974–5 was stemmed by a period of an uneasy so-called 'social contract' with the unions, negotiated by the Labour governments of Wilson and then James Callaghan in 1975–8. Unions agreed to moderate their wage demands in return for specified government policies geared to their needs, and especially to job protection. There were no serious strikes thereafter, until the so-called 'winter of discontent' in 1978–9, when a rash of strikes by public service workers, including even council grave-diggers, helped to ensure a Conservative election victory.

Thereafter, the unions continued to be assertive in 'right-to-work' demonstrations in protest at cuts in public spending and the high rate of unemployment. Not only traditionally vulnerable areas such as Scotland, Merseyside, and the north-east but even once thriving regions such as the West Midlands showed rates of joblessness amounting to over 20 per cent. In the steel industry, mighty plants like Consett, Shotton, and Corby were closed down for ever. More indirectly, the quality of life was impoverished by declining investment in health and educational services (including the universities) and by reduced expenditure on art and the environment. Britain now provided a classic example of the post-Keynesian phenomenon of 'stagflation', with industrial recession and high inflation at one and the same time.

Northern Ireland

These economic pressures led to severe strains being placed on the stability of society in the seventies. They fuelled other social, communal, or ethnic tensions already much in evidence. The most disturbing case was still Northern Ireland, where deep-seated racial and religious animosities between Protestants and Roman Catholics were aggravated by the highest rate of unemployment in the United Kingdom. Throughout the seventies, the state of Northern Ireland became more and more alarming. The success of the civil rights movement dislodged the old Unionist ascendancy; the Stormont assembly was wound up in 1972 in favour of direct rule by Westminster. But renewed violence by the IRA was paralleled by the aggressive anti-papist demagogy of the Reverend Ian Paisley.

The end of Stormont certainly brought communal peace no nearer. Troops continued to patrol the Bogside and the Falls Road. There were tense border incidents between Ulster and the Irish Republic to the south, from where the IRA derived funds and weapons. On occasion, the endemic violence of Northern Ireland stretched across the sea in the form of terrifying bomb attacks on English cities, and even assassinations of politicians. One of the Queen's relatives, the distinguished admiral and statesman, Lord Mountbatten, was murdered, blown up on his yacht by an IRA bomb.

A new effort to involve the Dublin government in the affairs of Northern Ireland directly, the first since 1922, came with the Anglo-Irish Hillsborough Agreement, concluded between the British prime minister, Margaret Thatcher, and the Irish Fine Gael premier, Garret FitzGerald, in November 1985. But this led to bitter protests from Unionists in Ulster, who then boycotted Westminster. A genuine all-Ireland spirit of unity in that unhappy island remained far off. The age-old racial feuds of Ireland were not yet pacified. Guns were freely available for both communities. Repeated acts of violence, including an abortive mortar attack by the IRA on 10 Downing Street in February 1991, drove the point home for the general public.

Nationalism, Race Relations, and Social Unrest

Other tensions of the period were less violent but equally disturbing. Scottish and Welsh nationalists continued to express themselves, though usually in constitutional form. After the failure of 'devolution' measures in 1979, Celtic nationalism seemed to be in retreat, but in Wales especially there continued to be much political and cultural conflict. The defence of the Welsh language still attracted much passionate loyalty, and even threats of fasts unto death by angry patriots. English people who owned a 'second home' in the Welsh countryside sometimes found it burned down by local incendiarists. Pressure for governmental devolution remained powerful in Scotland, fuelled by the relative decline of its economic base in the 1980s. Wales and Scotland, however, remained, on balance, peaceful societies, less torn apart by nationalist anguish than their Celtic neighbour across the sea.

More alarming were the troubles afflicting the large black community, much of it resident in poor, dilapidated ghetto areas in large cities.

There were sporadic troubles in the Notting Hill area of London and the St Paul's district of Bristol. In the summer of 1981 it seemed for a time that Britain was experiencing the full horrors of race riots on the American pattern, as black youths in the Toxteth area of Liverpool and the Brixton district of south London engaged in prolonged rioting, all faithfully recorded (and perhaps whipped up) by television reporting. Another violent flare-up saw disturbances on the Broadwater Farm housing estate in Tottenham, north London, and the murder of a policeman there, apparently by black youths. A lack of trust between the immigrant community and the police force was one notable aspect of these events. With unemployment especially serious for young black people and a pervasive background of discrimination in jobs, housing, and social opportunity, the relations between the races were a mounting cause for concern and alarm.

Other troubles piled up. Some examples of trade union protest, for instance the demonstrations against the Grunwick works in north London, seemed to go far beyond the usual limits of industrial protest in the intimidation that characterized them. Football matches and other sporting occasions were scarred by mindless violence by teenage spectators. Britain's traditional stability appeared, therefore, increasingly under fire from many sources. An American congressman gloomily observed that Britain was becoming as 'ungovernable as Chile', an alarming parallel for Americans.

This proved to be an absurd exaggeration. Few societies would have survived high unemployment, rising inflation, and public retrenchment with as much equanimity as did the British. Despite evidence of hallowed institutions being treated with less than their historic respect – Oxford University being subjected to 'sit-ins'; police, judges, Church leaders (and football referees) failing to sustain their former authority; even members of the royal family being subjected to public criticism or harassment – the broad fabric of institutional and civic life held firm. But, without doubt, the points of friction and potential dissolution were so numerous that age-old sanctions and restraints needed to be re-examined and redefined for British civilization to survive at all.

Europe

During this period of some turmoil, Britain's view of the outside world underwent a phase of introspection. In practice, a deep psychology of insularity dictated popular attitudes, as it had frequently done since 1918. The formal alliance with the Americans in NATO continued, but attracted little passionate commitment. Indeed, the temporary revival in the late 1970s of the Campaign for Nuclear Disarmament, a singularly peaceful form of protest, suggested that the dependence of this alliance on a mounting arsenal of nuclear weapons of a quite horrific kind still aroused public disquiet. The proposed Cruise missiles aroused more. After much diplomatic infighting, Britain entered the European Common Market in 1973.

A unique referendum in 1975 saw a large majority, almost two-thirds in all, recording its support for British membership. But 'Europe' attracted affection largely in non-political contexts. Continental package holidays, the popularity of Continental cars and food products, and European football matches did not make the British love their neighbours across the Channel any more fervently. British attitudes towards the Common Market continued after 1975 to be governed by sullen hostility; opinion polls recorded consistent opposition to membership of the European Economic Community (EEC). In any case, an organization which consisted largely of a massive, anonymous, bureaucratic juggernaut, with scant democratic constraint, located far away in Brussels and Strasbourg could hardly win public love in as independent a nation as Britain. The linking of the Common Market with higher food prices, butter mountains, wine lakes, and the like was widely condemned, inevitably so by a people which had known a policy of cheap food since the repeal of the Corn Laws in 1846. The British were reluctant Europeans as they were reluctant Atlanticists.

On the other hand, there were many signs by the later eighties that the British were becoming more reconciled to the fact of membership of the European community was bringing economic benefits, and that anti-Europeanism was diminishing. By the June 1987 general election, the Labour Party no longer proposed to negotiate British withdrawal from the EEC, especially since the latter now included socialist governments in France, Spain, and Greece. The agreement concluded in 1986 between Thatcher and President Mitterrand of France, to complete a high-speed rail tunnel under the English Channel to link Britain and France, a tunnel first operating in late 1993, was a dramatic indication of at least a partial retreat from British isolationism.

Britain agreed to enter the European Single Market in 1986, a momentous change. Finally, after much internal argument in her Cabinet, Thatcher was forced to enter the European Exchange Rate Mechanism (ERM) in October 1990. Nevertheless the economic and political relationship with Europe remained a deeply divisive issue at several levels of the Conservative party and government. It played a major part in Thatcher being forced to step down as prime minister in November 1990, after over eleven years in power.

The Commonwealth and the Falklands

Commonwealth sentiment still retained some force, with the queen as its figurehead. Yet the Commonwealth ties were becoming more and more intangible, too. Whether in the forms of black immigrants into British cities or of arguments over how to respond to apartheid in South Africa, they could produce friction rather than goodwill. Meanwhile the agreement with China in 1989 to withdraw the British presence in Hong Kong eight years later confirmed the irreversible retreat from a world role.

The withdrawal from empire continued apace with little public resentment. Economic and military weakness dictated a policy of controlled retreat. The most difficult surviving problem was that of Southern Rhodesia, where a racial holocaust was threatened in a land adjacent to South Africa with its apartheid system. In a dramatic reversal, Thatcher's Conservative government granted total self-government to Rhodesia (renamed Zimbabwe) in December 1979; the protests of white settlers were ignored. Parliament and public greeted this imperial retreat with a fanfare of acclamation. The spirit of Kipling and Cecil Rhodes had finally been exorcized. It seemed unlikely that empire would disturb the British psyche any further.

Then, quite unexpectedly, the distant, barren outpost of the Falkland Islands was invaded by the Argentines (who claimed them as 'the Malvinas') in late March 1982. The British government responded vigorously in the face of a huge public outcry. The two remaining aircraft-carriers and dozens of other war vessels, many fighter planes, and 10,000 troops were assembled in a task force and dispatched 8,000 miles away to the stormy seas of the South Atlantic. In a swift and successful campaign, much helped by American technical assistance, the islands were soon recaptured; the Union Jack again flew in Port Stanley on 14 June.

The Falklands War was immensely popular; dissidents, CND or otherwise, were unable to gain a fair hearing. At the same time, it seemed improbable that a war to retain these distant and almost valueless outposts, scarcely known to British people before the fighting began other than from postage stamps, would encourage a revived mystique of imperial grandeur. There was no more popular anxiety to commit naval strength or financial resources to the South Atlantic after the war than there had been before. What the Falklands episode possibly did was to confirm a rising tide of impatient insularity amongst the British people. In the face of international scepticism, Britain could still display great-power status, and demonstrate its military, naval, and technological superiority over a military dictatorship such as the Argentine republic. National pride was revived.

Domestic Unrest and Political Polarization

But the jingoism of the Falklands petered out almost as soon as it began. Britain returned to the familiar domestic scene of strikes, economic decline, and social discontent, exemplified by a bitter miners' strike from March 1984, which lasted a whole year. There were violent clashes between the police and miners' pickets. However, the National Union of Mineworkers was itself divided, with important Midlands' coalfields continuing to work, and the result was a profound defeat for the NUM and the closure of many more pits.

The power of the miners to coerce a British government into submission, a major feature of history and folklore since the First World War, was no longer apparent when coal was less essential to Britain's energy supplies, and with oil, gas, electricity, and nuclear power readily available. The miners' strike, however, was followed by a series of strikes by white-collar and public service workers, notably a lengthy dispute by Britain's school teachers which led to much disruption in schools in England and Wales in 1985-7.

The problems of the early eighties were intensified by a Conservative government under Thatcher which seemed to be the most right-wing that Britain had known in the twentieth century. At the same time, the Labour Party, with Tony Benn spearheading a grass-roots movement towards fundamentalist socialism, appeared to be moving equally far to the left. Consensus seemed to have disappeared. Commentators quoted W.B. Yeats to the effect that 'the best lacked all conviction and the worst were full of passionate intensity'. Some found refuge in a new political party formed by dissident right-wing members of the Labour Party; this was the Social Democratic Party, committed to Keynes-style economic centrism, to an incomes policy, Europeanism, and the nuclear deterrent. Remarkably, despite much fatalism about the economy, the June 1983 general election provided an immense triumph for Thatcher and the Conservatives. They captured 397 seats, as against 209 for a visibly declining Labour Party, 17 for the Liberals, and only 6 for the SDP.

Renewed fears that moderate middle-ground opinion would be swept away in the maelstrom were somewhat assuaged by other, more hopeful developments. The economic changes in the country were not without compensation. In part, they were the result of a beneficial change in the national economy, with Britain becoming self-sufficient in North Sea oil, and thus in a unique position of strength in its energy base. The balance of payments suddenly moved (until 1986) into a large and continuing surplus. This also meant that the dominance of manufacturing industry in the British economy would not be paramount henceforth. Certainly the technological wonders of oil, electronics, and aerospace, of Concorde, the Humber Bridge, the High-Speed Train, the Channel Tunnel, and the computerized microchip age suggested that the native reserves of innovation and scientific ingenuity had not run dry.

In the mid-eighties, there were many signs, too, that these developments were helping to generate a renewal of affluence, at least for southern England, parts of the Midlands, and East Anglia, the last an area of particular growth. Towns like Swindon and Basingstoke surged ahead. The British economy began to advance rapidly and reached a rate of 4 per cent growth in early 1987, assisted by the fall in the value of the pound and of some imported commodities. It was noticeable that this advance rested less on Britain's traditional strength in manufacturing, which continued to lag far below pre-1970 levels of production, than on financial services, credit, investment, and a consumer boom.

A notable event here was the so-called 'Big Bang' in the City of London, 27 October 1986, which replaced the age-old spectacle of jobbers milling on the Stock Exchange floor with an almost invisible, highly sophisticated computer-based network for dealers. This reflected the

10. The North Sea oil rig *Sea Quest*. Britain discovered oil reserves in the North Sea in 1969. The first oil was extracted in 1975 and by mid-1978 nine fields in the British sector were in production. By 1980 Britain was self-sufficient in oil and had become an oil exporter, with powerful beneficial results for the balance of payments. North Sea gas was another major source of energy

new internationalism of the capital market. It also contributed, incidentally, to repairing decades of neglect and dereliction in adjacent areas of London's East End. The social phenomenon of the 'yuppy' (young upwardly mobile professional), a money-making youth engaged in stock-broking, investment, or merchant banking, was widely discussed and often deplored.

For many British citizens, life suddenly appeared easier after the crises of the seventies and early eighties. Home ownership continued to spread until, by the end of 1987, two-thirds of the population owned their own home. Share-owning also became more widespread. The government's policy of 'privatizing' state-owned enterprises such as the telecommunications system, British Gas, Britoil, and the airports (with water and electricity to follow at the end of the decade) helped towards this last end. Conversely, the trade unions appeared to be declining in public esteem and even more in membership, which slumped from around 13 million in 1980 to 9 million in 1987 and to scarcely 6 million by 1999.

Cultural Developments

The land was not proving to be culturally barren or intellectually unadventurous at this time. British novelists and dramatists remained remarkably creative. Several leading British architects – James Stirling, Norman Foster, Richard Rogers (builder of the Pompidou Centre in Paris) – achieved international renown. The British musical scene was never more flourishing than in the 1980s, with London plausibly claimed to be the musical capital of the world, and important new orchestral and operatic developments in Leeds, Cardiff, and elsewhere. British weekly literary periodicals remained of high quality. The BBC remained a major communications agency, though much distracted by disputes with the Thatcher government, and weakened by falling morale and revenue. Universities still maintained a flow of creative achievement in the arts and pure and applied science, including medicine, despite a policy of government cuts imposed from 1981 onwards.

One American commentator, Bernard Nossiter, had even claimed in the late seventies that the apparent economic rundown and unemployment in Britain masked something more positive – a deliberately creative use of leisure in which the British middle and skilled working class rebelled against the norms of ever-increasing mass production, and opted for greater freedom from the drudgery of automated labour. This view was probably too optimistic and ignored long-held traditions in antique working practices and managerial inertia, which held the economy, and to some extent society, in thrall.

In addition, the material base on which British culture rested was threatened by a renewed failure in technological innovation and enterprise. The problems of British universities and research institutes aroused great concern in the mid-eighties, with the 'brain drain' of gifted young scientists across the Atlantic. Two hundred years after the dawn of the Industrial Revolution, the British were still strangely reluctant to modernize and promote their scientific genius. Yet, despite this glaring weakness, British talents were not necessarily unequipped to cope with the new stresses of sociological upheaval and relative industrial weakness, any more than with the burdens of commercial leadership and international power in past centuries.

The 'Two Nations'

These and other developments helped give a new lease of life to the Conservative government of Margaret Thatcher. In the June 1987 general election, despite a more vigorous Labour campaign under a new leader, Neil Kinnock, the Conservatives again won an easy victory, with 375 seats as against 219 for Labour and only 22 for a flagging and disintegrating Liberal/Social Democrat Alliance. Thatcher thus became the first prime minister since Lord Liverpool in 1812–27 to win three successive general elections, an extraordinary achievement. The Conservatives made much in the campaign of their claims to have restored national prosperity, and also to be reliable protectors of national security. Labour's policy of unilateral nuclear disarmament did not command wide support. In thriving southern England, the party appeared divided, dated, and unelectable.

On the other hand, the regional gulf in Britain revealed by the election returns was very plain. The sweeping Conservative gains came in the south and the Midlands. They lost ground in the industrial cities of the north; there was a 5 per cent swing to Labour in Wales; and a 7.5 per cent swing in Scotland. There was much talk of a basic social divide in the land, between an increasingly prosperous and complacent south, and a decaying, declining north, with endemic unemployment, urban dereliction, and collapsing public services. The 'two nations' described in Benjamin Disraeli's novels in the 1840s were still much in evidence well over a century later.

Britain in the 1980s manifested a remarkable skein of elements of dissolution and stability, in fragile co-existence. The forces of disruption were evident enough. There were physical reminders in the troubles in Northern Ireland, in the industrial world, and in the black ghettos in the cities. There was the new challenge to the political consensus posed in their various guises by the neo-Marxist Labour left headed by Benn, by the racialist perversities of the quasi-Fascist National Front, and perhaps by the patrician detachment displayed at times by some Social Democrats. Traditional relationships – the young towards their parents, 'feminist' wives to their husbands, workers to their employers and union leaders, students to their teachers, citizens to the custodians of law and order – seemed to be in flux. *Is Britain Dying?* was one evocative book title in 1979. British stability was too often expressed, by contrast, in an almost religious reverence for ancient forms and ancestor worship, as in the veneration of the royal family, or the ambiguous notion of 'heritage', which often entailed a distinctly selective and sentimental reading of British history.

Public instability was markedly reinforced by the disarray into which Thatcher's government lurched after the 1987 general election. For most of the decade, with its creed of monetarism, privatization, and the primacy of market forces; with its challenge to institutions such as the Church, the universities, and local government; with the almost invincible personal ascendancy of the prime minister herself, 'Thatcherism' seemed triumphant. But over the next three years it ran into severe difficulties. At home, some of its more radical proposals met with major opposition. Attempts to introduce market forces into education and even more into the National Health Service aroused great public anger. A proposal to abolish the system of household rates with a community charge (or 'poll tax') led to an upsurge of revolt across the nation. After all, freeborn Englishmen, headed by Wat Tyler, had rebelled against a poll tax back in 1381, and the memory of it remained in popular legend.

Most serious of all, the apparent revival in the economy began to lose credibility. The tax-cutting policy of the chancellor, Nigel Lawson, was now seen to have led to a huge balance of payments deficit, at £20 billion the worst figure on record. Unemployment rose sharply and the pound came under pressure. Worse still, the conquest of inflation, the government's main boast, was now threatened by a consumer credit and spending boom. The bank rate soared to 15 per cent, and the impact was felt by every mortgaged home-owner in the land. To make matters worse, Lawson, locked in bitter argument with the prime minister over European policy, resigned.

Thatcher herself now became increasingly unpopular. Her intensely personal, imperious style of leadership now seemed more of a liability. Her reputation for 'strength' in foreign affairs, dating from the Falklands War, also seemed less credible, especially with repeated rows over monetary union with Britain's European partners. At the same time, the Labour Party, responding to Kinnock's 'new realism' became increasingly moderate and therefore more electable. It dropped its commitment to mass nationalization and unilateral nuclear disarmament, and its hostility towards Europe, and turned on the hard-left Bennite remnants in the process. In the summer of 1990 it seemed that a sea change in British politics might be at hand.

The Fall of Thatcher

In the autumn, the transformation duly occurred. Faced with Cabinet resignations, by-election losses, and difficulties over Europe and the economy, Thatcher seemed beleaguered as never before. She was then challenged for the party leadership (in effect, for the premiership) in November by Michael Heseltine, one of the many former Cabinet colleagues who had resigned from her government. Although Thatcher won the first ballot (204 votes to Heseltine's 152), the opposition to her within her party was sufficient to force her to resign. Like Lloyd George in 1922 and Chamberlain in 1940, it was the Tory backbenchers, not the voters, who brought her down. In the second ballot, the victor was John Major, the little-known chancellor of the Exchequer, and a man of apparently moderate views. He thus became prime minister, to guide the nation through the transition from the storms of 'Thatcherism' to a more consensual social and political order.

Chapter 7
Towards the Millennium

The fall of Thatcher in 1990, like that of Lloyd George in 1922, was a traumatic event. As with the departure of that earlier leader, it seemed to usher in a period of greater tranquillity – Major spoke of 'a nation at ease with itself'. As a unifying move, he brought Thatcher's main adversary, Heseltine, into his Cabinet. For a while, there was a quieter phase. The unpopular poll tax was scrapped. British involvement in the Gulf War in February 1991, when its armoured troops and jet fighters were prominent in helping the Americans and other 'coalition' forces to drive Saddam Hussein's Iraqi armies out of Kuwait, shored up the government's popularity for a time, even if there was no 'Falklands factor' now to boost the Tory cause.

Above all, John Major appeared to make progress in reconciling the divisions in his party over Europe. In the negotiations over the Maastricht treaty in December 1991, which spurred on European integration, including a common currency that was to start in 1999, the British government appeared to achieve a diplomatic success. It won from its European partners an 'opt-out' from both future monetary union and also the 'social chapter' of workers' rights and a minimum wage. A facade of Conservative unity was successfully maintained.

On the other hand, the basic difficulties of Thatcher's later period still remained in full. In particular, the economy remained in recession. This time it was the middle classes of middle England who were conspicuously suffering, from job insecurity, dear mortgages, negative equity, and falling house prices. A new privatization, of the railway system, proved to be deeply controversial.

The 1992 General Election and its Aftermath

With all these problems confronting their natural supporters and their endless difficulties over Europe, it was generally expected that the Conservatives would finally lose to Labour in the general election of April 1992 – certainly that is what the opinion polls said. But they were simply wrong. John Major projected himself effectively as a plain, honest citizen without artifice. He won an unexpected victory, with the Conservatives winning 336 seats to Labour's 271 and the Liberal Democrats' 20. The government gained the support of 'Essex man', the patriotic, *Sun*-reading, skilled or semi-skilled worker in new towns such as Basildon. In fact, with 41.85 per cent of the votes to Labour's 34.16 per cent, the Conservatives had done much better than their tally of seats suggested. Their total of 14,200,000 votes was their highest ever. It seemed that the electors did not really trust either Labour or its leader, Kinnock, for economic competence. Labour to most electors still seemed the class-conscious party of a dying past, not a prosperous future. The Conservatives, having won four general elections running, the best performance since the nineteenth-century Whig-Liberals after the repeal of the Corn Laws, seemed destined for a further period of comfortable ascendancy.

Yet, in fact, the election was to bring a prolonged phase of division and torment that tore the Conservatives asunder. The collapse began on 'Black Wednesday', 16 September 1992, a traumatic day from which neither party nor premier was to recover. After intense pressure on sterling, Britain was forced to leave the European ERM and to devalue the pound against all major currencies. It was a shattering blow for Major and his chancellor, Norman Lamont, which destroyed at a stroke the Conservatives' reputation for competent economic management. They slumped massively in the opinion polls; Labour's lead, which rose at times even to a record margin of over 30 per cent, remained immense for the next four and a half years. There seemed little that the government could do to recover.

Economic revival brought the voters cut-backs and higher taxes. Kenneth Clarke succeeded Lamont as chancellor in 1993 and things slowly improved. There were other unpopular policies. The privatization of industries and utilities, the flagship of Thatcherite policies, lost its sheen. The public saw privatized trains which did not run on time, and privatized water services which led to shortages during dry summer months and huge salary increases for the company executives.

Northern Ireland and Europe

There was, indeed, some progress in Northern Ireland for a time. Major succeeded in negotiating a Downing Street agreement with the Irish prime minister in late 1993; the following year Sinn Fein declared a cease-fire which lasted for almost two years. Peace returned to the troubled streets of Belfast and the British army scaled down its presence. But a massive bomb blast in Canary Wharf in east London in February 1996 meant that the fragile peace was over for the moment. The political gulf between Protestant loyalists and Catholic Nationalists remained as wide as it had been ever since the partition of Ireland back in 1922. Major, like all his predecessors, had not managed to overcome the ancestral sectarian divisions and bitterness of Northern Ireland.

Above all, the Conservative Party was plagued by relations with Europe. The Maastricht treaty of 1991 proved to be not a platform for harmony but a ticking time-bomb that led inexorably to electoral disaster. Under leaders like Macmillan and Heath, the Conservatives had always been the more pro-European party since the 1950s, while Labour had been far more hostile. Now the positions were totally reversed. Labour felt wholly committed to a British role at the centre of Europe, including the social chapter and the minimum wage, which the unions warmly endorsed, while the Conservatives were ripped apart as the Euro-scepticism or Europhobia of Thatcher's later period built up into a kind of frenzy.

It was no longer the siren call of empire that promoted anti-European sentiment, but threats to British national independence. Maastricht, with its perceived challenge to the sovereignty of the Crown in parliament, with its pressure towards a European superstate and a 'Euro' currency which would wipe out the historic primacy of the pound sterling, became the source of massive contention. The Conservative Cabinet was as divided over Europe as a previous Cabinet in 1903–5 had been over tariff reform and empire. Major seemed as helpless and indecisive now as Arthur Balfour then – and in 1906 the outcome had been a massive electoral defeat.

Battle raged year after year in the Commons between different Conservative factions over Maastricht and Europe generally. Party divisions led to huge losses in by-elections and local government elections until the party at the grass roots seemed close to extinction. In the European elections of June 1994, Labour won 64 seats to the Conservatives' 18 and the Liberal Democrats' 2; after that, things got worse still. A variety of disputes about food added to the turmoil. Veal, lamb, and the right to fish in British territorial waters were all said to be threatened by Brussels. Worst of all, the advent of BSE, a new disease among cattle which led to a few people dying and posed a major threat to public health, led to the European Union (EU), headed by Germany, banning British beef exports to the Continent. It was the result of Thatcherite policies of deregulating animal feed, but it led to a massive outcry amongst British beef farmers, Tory backbenchers, and Europhobes in general. In the summer of 1996 there was a revival of anti-German prejudice of a kind unknown since the 1950s. The tabloid press, especially the Murdoch-owned *Sun*, fanned populist xenophobia.

But the beef ban went on. Major, goaded almost beyond reason by his Europhobe critics, actually resigned the party leadership in May 1995 and defeated a right-wing challenger, John Redwood, with some ease. But the episode only served to emphasize Major's long-term political weakness.

Sleaze and Corruption

The tone and style of public life, perhaps more than the substance of policy, added to a mood of disillusionment and cynicism in the mid-1990s. The government plunged into an extraordinary morass of sexual or financial scandals reminiscent of the early 1960s, an earlier period of lengthy one-party rule. An obscure word, 'sleaze', dominated public perceptions of political life, fanned remorselessly by a tabloid press that turned against Major and his government. A series of minor government ministers was involved in a variety of sexual peccadilloes and had to resign. Even in an age of moral permissiveness, such behaviour was held to be politically unacceptable. It was especially so for a party which had unwisely proclaimed its attachment to 'family values' and its urge moralistically to 'go back to basics', a phrase in whose very ambiguity perils lurked.

Worse still, a growing range of covert links between business and finance and Tory politicians appeared to suggest a deep rot of corruption in Westminster. Ministers or backbenchers were shown to have received undeclared payments from private firms or intermediate lobbyists. A number of ministerial resignations followed.

There were also serious moral problems with aspects of policy. Cabinet ministers were publicly censured in the Scott inquiry for misleading or deceiving Parliament in the sale of arms to Iraq down to 1991 (arms used against British troops in the Gulf War), while the Nolan Committee censured the standards of public life and called for far greater transparency.

By the standards of American or perhaps Italian politics, the transgressions seemed relatively small-scale. In British terms, where the rooting out of corrupt practices had begun in the late eighteenth century, they seemed shocking. The government appeared casual, if not corrupt, and Major a leader who either did not know or did not care about what was happening.

Public Disillusion

The atmosphere of Conservative decline and widespread 'sleaze' made the mid-nineties apparently a time of much public disillusion. Works of criticism like Will Hutton's *The State We're In* (1995) condemned the social inequality, centralization, and declining community sense in post-Thatcher Britain; Hutton called for a revived citizenship and republican solidarity. Many institutions were now under fire. Even the monarchy found itself facing a wave of popular criticism unknown since Regency times. It was fuelled by private family troubles such as the separation and later divorce of Prince Charles and Princess Diana, and by criticism over the monarch's wealth, lifestyle, and inability to adapt to modern times. A fire at Windsor Castle led to massive criticism when public funds were used to repair the damage. In 1992, the Queen spoke of the year as having been 'an *annus horribilis*'. Republicanism showed some limited signs of making headway, just as it was doing in Australia.

Elsewhere faith in the City of London was undermined by the Robert Maxwell pensions scandal and troubles in Lloyd's Insurance. The criminal justice system showed up police abuses in cases such as the Birmingham Six where evidence had been tampered with. The Home Office was criticized for attacks on civil liberties and political interference with the law.

There was also much public disgust with the state of British society. In east London, elegant postmodernist tower blocks, an ecological park, and a marina built by the Docklands Corporation around Canary Wharf contrasted starkly with young homeless people sleeping rough in the Strand or Lincoln's Inn Fields. Disparities in wealth, income, health, and lifestyle had grown ever-wider. Long-departed diseases like tuberculosis returned to haunt the poor, quite apart from newer scourges like Aids. There were other sources of instability, too. Family breakdown went on apace: one marriage in three broke down and Britain had the highest divorce rate in the EU, higher even than the Scandinavian countries. There was long-term youth unemployment in areas like Merseyside, many troubled housing estates, and an endemic drug culture in urban areas, portrayed in the film *Trainspotting*, based on a disturbing novel by the Edinburgh writer Irvine Welsh. British society, never more affluent, seemed spiritually impoverished and socially divided.

Growing Prosperity

Yet in many ways, this feeling was unbalanced and the despair exaggerated. In spite of all its problems, Major's Britain was increasingly prosperous and most of its citizens content with their lot. Despite disturbing evidence in the Stephen Lawrence murder case of racial prejudice among the police, ethnic minorities had made progress after the racial disturbances of the Thatcher years. Family incomes rose as a majority of women, married as well as single, now found employment; domestic servants such as nannies or childminders rose in number for the first time since the Edwardian era. Amongst the young, entry into university rose sharply to include a third of the age-group, while part-time or 'continuing' education became widespread. At the other end of the age scale, the expectation of life rose steadily (to 77 for women), while early retirement on personal pensions often meant a more comfortable old age.

Foreign holidays were commonplace, helped by the Channel Tunnel being opened for road and rail in 1994. The vast majority of households had comforts such as central heating, microwaves, videos, or personal computers. Information technology, including the Internet, meant that more and more people were able to work from their own homes and enjoyed a hugely enhanced access to knowledge. There were over 12 million mobile phones. City life showed a recovery, with towns such as Glasgow, Cardiff, Newcastle, or Leeds booming, with more cheerful pubs and more cosmopolitan restaurants and cafés. The excitement of gambling on the National Lottery (which generated much money for charitable causes) was very popular. Leisure activities reflected a wider affluence. Football in particular became hugely successful, with immense funding from satellite television and star foreign players imported from the Continent or South America. Among other things, the success of black footballers, athletes, or cricketers materially helped in race relations.

Much of British culture remained vigorously alive. London was still a great literary centre; architects like Norman Foster and Richard Rogers were internationally celebrated. Foster, symbolically, designed the rebuilt Berlin *Reichstag*, opened in late 1999. The cinema became especially thriving and creative, with multiscreen theatres attracting many more filmgoers. Successful films ranged from a historical classic like *The Madness of King George* (made by Channel Four television) to *The Full Monty* (1997), a bracing account of six unemployed Sheffield steelworkers who turned their talents to striptease. The press was full of the vitality of British art and design; pop icons like the Spice Girls testified both to 'girl power' and to a new ersatz patriotism. There was brief talk of 'Cool Britannia' and the country being a market leader in popular fashion as it had been in the heyday of the Beatles and the 'swinging sixties'. As the economy began to recover with an export-led growth in 1995–7, commentators puzzled over the apparent absence of a 'feel-good factor'. The public mood appeared strangely downbeat.

New Labour

Politics were the source of much of this disillusion. It also seemed to be politics that brought a hope of revival. The Labour Party, apparently doomed to permanent opposition as the symbol of the old socialism and union troubles of the past, unexpectedly became the hope of a better world. The recovery had begun under Kinnock when left-wing policies were abandoned. His successor, John Smith, continued a process of modernization by cutting down the power of the unions and the introduction of 'one man, one vote' into party conference.

But the real change came after Smith died in 1994. His successor, Tony Blair, a 42-year-old public-school and Oxford-educated barrister who jettisoned old ideologies, led a dramatic revival. Giving an attractive impression of youthful freshness and a sense of the new, he became the most successful party leader in modern British history. He spoke not of 'Labour' but of 'New Labour'. He appealed less to the older working classes of Labour's heartland than to the mortgaged home-owning middle classes of middle England. He spoke the language of British patriotism and brandished the Union flag. Britain, he declared, was essentially a young country. He projected himself with a remarkably sophisticated apparatus of modern communications technology to keep the party 'on message' and elevate the role of the leader. Major was taunted by Blair in the Commons: 'You follow your party, I lead mine.'

New Labour was much more inclusive. Blair appealed openly to business leaders in the Confederation of British Industry (CBI); he courted the Murdoch press which had traduced his party in the past; he even spoke well of Thatcher's achievements in privatizing nationalized industries, spreading home-ownership, and ending the stranglehold of the unions. His model appeared to be not the old Labour Party which had spanned the century from Keir Hardie to Callaghan, but the 'market socialism' of Australian Labour or perhaps the American Democratic Party under President Bill Clinton.

The effect was a remarkably undoctrinaire Labour Party which rejected the State planning, the nationalization, the universalized welfare benefits, the income redistribution, and the links with the unions which had characterized Attlee's party in 1945. Blair announced himself with a successful campaign for Labour to throw out Clause Four, the commitment to nationalization, in early 1995. Buoyed up by Tory failures and an immense lead in the polls, he dominated British politics.

The 1997 General Election

The effect was seen in the 1997 general election. The opinion polls this time were amply confirmed. The Conservatives suffered an electoral débâcle worse even than 1945 or 1906, indeed their worst since the duke of Wellington had resisted the great Reform Act in 1832. There was a 10.9 per cent swing to Labour, which won 419 seats against the Conservatives' 165, with the Liberals capturing 46, their best score since the 1920s. Five Cabinet ministers lost their seats; suburban seats in England swung massively to Labour, including Thatcher's seat in Finchley. The major cities all went Labour, while Scotland and Wales returned not one Conservative between them.

Another remarkable feature of the election was the election of no fewer than 120 women MPs; over 100 of them were Labour, all middle-class, while the trade union element in the party largely disappeared. It was one of the most remarkable electoral upheavals in British history, a delayed reaction against Conservative rule which had been welling up since the poll tax revolt against Thatcher ten years earlier. Blair thus became at 44 the youngest premier since Victorian times, and immediately imposed a sense of personal authority.

Labour's transition to high office was remarkably smooth. The economy had been improving rapidly of late; here was the first Labour government in history to come to power without being met by a financial crisis. The new chancellor followed a prudent financial policy, carrying out a pre-election pledge to maintain Conservative taxing and spending limits. The Stock Exchange boomed to new levels in 1998. The index of share prices rose from 4,300 in May 1997 to over 6,800 in January 2000. There was a mood of caution, even conservatism in domestic policies, especially in whittling down the welfare system so as to reduce dependency on the state, but protests from the left were brushed aside. The under-funding of the health service provoked much controversy. There was a deliberate policy of friendship towards business, a tough stance on law and order, and the first charges for university tuition, all of these remarkable for a government of the centre left. On the other hand, family credits, enhanced provision for children and pensioners, and a minimum wage for workers indicated some redistribution and a genuinely progressive agenda.

On Europe, the government seemed much more positive than its predecessor. But Blair was no more inclined to join a single European currency in the first wave than Major had been. His instincts seemed transatlantic as much as European. In Northern Ireland, however, the government did appear to achieve a rare political breakthrough after decades of violence. Sinn Fein and Unionist politicians were brought together around the same table, and on Good Friday, April 1998, they came together to reach an agreement. It would involve setting up a 108-member elected assembly on the lines of that proposed for Scotland; a cross-border Ministerial Council for ministers from Dublin and Belfast to handle security and other matters; and a British–Irish Council of the Isles. It appeared to be much the closest that Ulster's politicians had come to a meeting of minds since the partition of Ireland in 1922, and represented among other things a remarkable diplomatic achievement for Blair. The agreement was endorsed by a majority of over 71 per cent (including a majority of Protestants) in the referendum held in Northern Ireland a month later. After much difficulty over the removal of weapons, the Northern Ireland Assembly began operating in November 1999 with Sinn Fein ministers holding office under the Unionist leader, David Trimble, in a historic new development, though it was soon to be suspended.

The potential federalism inherent in the Northern Irish agreement chimed in with one domestic area where the Labour government did prove remarkably radical. In a tranche of proposed constitutional reforms, it voted to remove hereditary peers from the House of Lords, with only a rump of 92 remaining in the year 2000. More remarkably still, it introduced referendums for Scottish and Welsh devolution in September 1997. Scotland voted overwhelmingly for a Scottish Parliament with taxing powers; Wales by contrast endorsed an elected assembly by the narrowest of margins. The outcome, perhaps, would be a dramatic change in the centralized governance of the United Kingdom as it had existed since the Act of Union in 1707. It might even, some speculated, remain united no longer. The advent of a Scottish Parliament in 1999, with a minority Labour government but strong SNP representation, along with British involvement in a much more integrated EU, seemed likely to generate further changes. Pluralism at home and integration in Europe could lead to a much looser structure in which the roles of the law, Parliament, and Cabinet were transformed, to produce a very different view of the British identity. A few responded to this with a fierce kind of English nationalism. But most people, recognizing a post-imperial world, the information revolution, and a global economy, appeared to accept the prospect of major changes ahead with traditional equanimity.

Public Tranquillity

As the Blair government settled in, British people contemplated the advent of a new millennium. They appeared to do so in a mood of distinctly greater tranquillity, even self-confidence than had seemed likely after Thatcher's fall from power. The economy had shown recovery; society (even in Northern Ireland) was more tranquil; gender equality was making progress; ethnic minorities were more widely integrated; the Scots and the Welsh busied themselves constructively in preparations for devolution. Britain seemed to have found a style and a leadership with which, for the moment, it felt comfortable.

11. Mourners outside Kensington Palace prior to the funeral of Princess Diana, September 1997

Certainly there were ample signs of massive upheavals in recent decades. The interaction of classes, genders, and generations, and social keystones like marriage, family, and parenthood, experienced massive strains and became less structured. Historic institutions could find it hard to cope. The Church of England had much difficulty in adapting itself to a secular age; issues like the ordination of women priests added to its anxieties. Religious observance was confined to a small minority. The nonconformist conscience was a relic of Victorian times, while the Catholic church was under fire for its views on issues such as abortion. Except in the furthest Calvinist recesses of the Scottish Western Isles, Sunday was a relaxed day for shopping, motoring, and mass sport.

The monarchy had been an even greater victim of recent turmoil. Many speculated that Prince Charles might not even inherit the throne when Queen Elizabeth II eventually died. But an extraordinary popular catharsis occurred on 31 August 1997 with the death in a car crash in Paris of Princess Diana, the divorced wife of Prince Charles. At her funeral, there was an outpouring of grief by a people for whom she had been both a glamorous show-business icon who dominated the tabloid press, and also a kind of establishment outsider who showed empathy with social victims such as Aids sufferers, the homeless, single mothers, and Asian minorities. Her funeral encouraged a renewed attachment to the monarchy, even if expressed in a more casual, less deferential manner.

In a way, Blair took her place, a beacon of authority rather than (as the princess was called at her funeral) a candle in the wind. The opinion polls recorded, in the face of much processed gloom in the media, a popular commitment to being British and a satisfaction with one's country not universal in the Western world. No one much wanted to emigrate. At the millennium in January 2000, a large plastic dome along the riverside arose at Greenwich. It was heir to the Crystal Palace of 1851 and the Festival Hall of 1951. It generated press criticism as they had once done, but without bitterness. Like the monarchy, the millennium could be used to reinforce a basic commitment to a civic culture to which newer immigrant citizens could also respond.

Conclusion

Britain in the years from 1914 to 2000 had gone through seismic transformations. Yet it was recognizably the same society. Despite two world wars, the mass unemployment of the thirties, and the social turmoil of the seventies and eighties, the face of Great Britain, like Snowdonia or Hardy's Egdon Heath, might show surface changes of light or pattern; but the underlying geology remained the same. In 2000 as in 1914 there remained a profound, non-exclusive sense of place. A loyalty to London (with its own elected mayor as of May 2000), to 'the north' or Tyneside or East Anglia or Cornwall, to the separate nationalities of Scotland or Wales was still a reality – indeed, with Scottish and Welsh devolution perhaps to be followed by extended civic government in English cities, a sense of definable local community might even become stronger.

The population remained intensely various, distinct, individual. In a largely urbanized society, the countryside retained a fierce (perhaps exaggerated) sense of its own needs and identity. Much of Britain in the late nineties was still the same relatively neighbourly society where people pursued their hobbies, cherished their gardens, and entertained in their own homes. Most powerfully of all, despite the rhetoric about 'a young country', the British retained a pride in their collective past – even if 'British history' (largely ignored in the Millennium Dome) might have to be redefined in a pluralist, polycultural sense to take account variously of Celtic devolution, Americanized popular culture, Commonwealth immigration, and membership of Europe.

Debates over the significance of Diana's death or the meaning of the millennium offered insights into this abiding folk memory. An awareness of the past shone through in innumerable local festivals, in the civility of old cathedral cities and spa towns, in the Welsh national *eisteddfod*, in the Highland games, even in the multi-ethnic Notting Hill carnival, now over 30 years old. Public institutions like Parliament embodied this sense of history. So, too, more painfully, did the sense of resolve generated by the crisis of war or external threat. In the mass media, historical or other productions on television or film revived the mystique of ancient identity. Popular polls in January 2000 decreed William Shakespeare to be man of the millennium.

In spite of decades of almost unbearable upheaval, Britain remained an organic, comparatively peaceful, close-knit society, capable of self-renewal. Its very forms of native protest often testified to an innate tolerance; a respect for individuality and eccentricity, including in difficult areas such as sexual preference; and a rejection of coercion and uniformity. The 'Liberty tree' was still being nurtured by environmental pressure groups in 1998. The eco-warrior 'Swampy' was a natural dissenting heir of the Levellers or Tom Paine. At the dawn of the new millennium, as in times of greater pomp and power in the past, the values of being British could still be affirmed and sustained. So might they be again, in centuries yet to unfold.

Further Reading

General

J. M. Brown and W. R. Louis (eds), *The Twentieth Century: The Oxford History of the British Empire*, vol. IV (Oxford, 1999).

P. Clarke, *Hope and Glory: Britain 1900–1990* (London, 1996).

T. O. Lloyd, *Empire to Welfare State. English History, 1906–1992* (4th edn, Oxford, 1993), a good general survey.

C. L. Mowat, *Britain between the Wars* (London, 1955), excellent on social and economic themes.

K. O. Morgan, *The People's Peace: British History since 1945* (Oxford, 1999).

N. Tiratsoo (ed.), *From Blitz to Blair* (London, 1998).

Social and Economic

W. Ashworth, *An Economic History of Britain, 1870–1939* (London, 1960).

A. Cairncross, *Years of Recovery: British Economic Policy, 1945–51* (London, 1985), a fine study of the Attlee years.

J. R. C. Dow, *The Management of the British Economy, 1945–60* (Cambridge, 1964).

R. Floud and D. McCloskey (eds), *The Economic History of Britain since 1700*, vol. iii (Cambridge, 1994).

A. H. Halsey (ed.), *Trends in British Society since 1900* (London, 1971), comprehensive and factual.

J. Lewis, *Women in Britain since 1945* (London, 1992).

R. Lowe, *The Welfare State since 1945* (London, 1993).

R. McKibbin, *Culture and Classes: England 1918–1951* (Oxford, 1998).

A. Marwick, *The Deluge* (London, 1965), covers the effects of the First World War.

G. C. Peden, *British Economic and Social Policy: Lloyd George to Margaret Thatcher* (Deddington, 1985).

H. Pelling, *A History of British Trade Unionism* (2nd edn, London, 1971).

H. Perkin, *The Rise of Professional Society: England since 1880* (London, 1989).

E. H. Phelps Brown, *The Growth of British Industrial Relations, 1906–14* (London, 1963).

S. Pollard, *The Development of the British Economy, 1914–1980* (3rd edn, London, 1983).

J. Stevenson, *British Society, 1914–1945* (London, 1984).

Political

P. Addison, *The Road to 1945* (London, 1975), a stimulating account of consensus and conflict in wartime politics.

S. Beer, *Modern British Politics* (new edn, London, 1982), a stimulating thematic approach.

R. Blake, *The Conservative Party from Peel to Major* (new edn, London, 1997).

C. Hazlehurst, *Politicians at War, July 1914 to May 1915* (London, 1971).

D. Kavanagh, *Thatcherism and British Politics* (Oxford, 1984).

R. McKibbin, *The Evolution of the Labour Party, 1910–1924* (Oxford, 1983).

D. Marquand, *The Unprincipled Society* (London, 1988), a perceptive critique of the British political economy.

K. O. Morgan, *Labour in Power, 1945–1951* (Oxford, 1984).

K. O. Morgan, *Labour People: Leaders and Lieutenants, Hardie to Kinnock* (new edn, Oxford, 1992).

R. A. C. Parker, *Chamberlain and Appeasement* (London, 1993), a powerful reassessment.

M. Pugh, *The Making of Modern British Politics, 1867–1939* (London, 1982), a helpful survey for the student.

J. Ramsden, *An Appetite for Power* (London, 1998), the modern history of the Conservatives.

D. Reynolds, *Britannia Overruled: British Policy and World Power in the Twentieth Century* (London, 1991), a fine overview.

R. Skidelsky, *Politicians and the Slump* (London, 1968), the second Labour government.

T. Wilson, *The Downfall of the Liberal Party, 1914–1935* (London, 1966).

Biographies

R. Blake and R. Louis (eds), *Churchill* (Oxford, 1993), authoritative essays.

B. Brivati, *Hugh Gaitskell* (London, 1996).

A. Bullock, *The Life and Times of Ernest Bevin*, 3 vols (London, 1960, 1967, 1983).

J. Campbell, *Edward Heath* (London, 1993).

B. Crick, *George Orwell. A Life* (London, 1980).

D. Dilks, *Neville Chamberlain*, vol. i (Cambridge, 1984).

R. Foster, *W. B. Yeats: A Life*, vol. i (Oxford, 1997).

J. Harris, *William Beveridge* (Oxford, 1977).

K. Harris, *Attlee* (London, 1982).

C. Hussey, *The Life of Sir Edwin Lutyens* (London, 1950).

H. Lee, *Virginia Woolf* (London, 1996).

D. Marquand, *Ramsay MacDonald* (London, 1977).

K. O. Morgan, *Callaghan: A Life* (Oxford, 1997).

B. Pimlott, *Hugh Dalton* (London, 1985).

R. Skidelsky, *John Maynard Keynes*, vols i and ii (London, 1983, 1992)

H. Young, *One of Us* (London, 1989), on Margaret Thatcher.

Scotland, Ireland, and Wales

J. Davies, *A History of Wales* (London, 1993).

C. Harvie, *Scotland and Nationalism* (new edn, London, 1994).

C. Harvie, *No Gods and Precious Few Heroes: Scotland 1914–1980* (new edn, London, 1998).

J. Lee, *Ireland, 1922–1985: Politics and Society* (Cambridge, 1989).

F. S. L. Lyons, *Ireland since the Famine* (rev. edn, London, 1973), a definitive survey from the 1840s to the 1970s.

K. O. Morgan, *Rebirth of a Nation: Wales 1880–1980* (Oxford and Cardiff, 1981).

Culture and the Arts

G. Abraham, *The Concise Oxford History of Music* (Oxford, 1979).

B. Bergonzi (ed.), *The Twentieth Century: Sphere History of Literature in the English Language*, vol. vii (London, 1970).

D. Farr, *English Art, 1870–1940* (Oxford, 1978), including architecture.

B. Ford (ed.), *The Pelican Guide to English Literature*, vol. vii. *From James to Eliot* (rev. edn, London, 1983).

B. Ford (ed.), *The Pelican Guide to English Literature*, vol. viii. The Present (London, 1983).

B. Ford (ed.), *The Cambridge Guide to the Arts in Britain*, vol. viii (Cambridge, 1989), comprehensive.

J. Gross, *The Rise and Fall of the English Man of Letters* (London, 1969), a brilliant study.

R. Hewison, *In Anger: Culture and the Cold War* (London, 1981).

R. Hewison, *Too Much: Art and Society in the Sixties, 1960–1975* (London, 1988).

P. Kidson, P. Murray, and P. Thompson (eds), *A History of English Architecture* (London, 1979).

A. Marwick, *Culture in Britain since 1945* (London, 1991).

W. W. Robson, *Modern English Literature* (Oxford, 1970), the best brief account.

R. Samuel, *Theatres of Memory* (London, 1994).

P. Young, *A History of British Music* (London, 1967).

Chronology

1914	(28 June) Assassination of Archduke Ferdinand at Sarajevo (4 August) British Empire enters First World War
1915–16	Dardanelles expedition, ending in British withdrawal from Gallipoli
1916	Battle of the Somme; battle of Jutland; Lloyd George succeeds Herbert Asquith as prime minister
1917	Battle of Passchendaele
1918	Representation of the People Act enfranchies women aged 30 and over; end of First World War (11 November); Lloyd George coalition government returned in 'coupon election' (December)
1919	Treaty of Versailles establishes peace in Europe
1921	Miners seek support of dockers' and railwaymen's unions (the 'Triple Alliance') in major strike: on 'Black Friday' the dockers and railwaymen back down, and the alliance is broken; Lloyd George concludes treaty with Sinn Fein
1922	Fall of Lloyd George; Bonar Law heads Conservative government
1923	Stanley Baldwin becomes Conservative prime minister; general election
1924	(January) Ramsay MacDonald leads first Labour government (November) Conservatives return to office under Baldwin
1925	Britain goes back on the gold standard

1926	General Strike (3–12 May)
1929	General election; MacDonald leads second Labour government
1931	Financial crisis and run on the pound; Britain abandons the gold standard; MacDonald resigns and is returned in the election to head National government
1932	Ottawa Conference on imperial trade institutes protective tariffs
1935	Conservatives win general election: Baldwin succeeds MacDonald as prime minister; Hoare–Laval pact on Abyssinia; Government of India Act
1936	Death of King George V; abdication of Edward VIII: George VI becomes king
1937	Neville Chamberlain succeeds Baldwin as Conservative prime minister
1938	Chamberlain meets Adolf Hitler at Berchtesgaden, Bad Godesberg, and Munich
1939	British guarantee to Poland; British Empire declares war on Germany (3 September)
1940	Winston Churchill succeeds Chamberlain as prime minister; withdrawal from Dunkirk; battle of Britain
1941	Luftwaffe Blitz continues on many British cities; Soviet Union and United States enter the war
1942	Loss of Singapore; Montgomery's victory at El Alamein; battle of Stalingrad; Beveridge Report on social insurance
1943	Successful campaign in North Africa; Anglo-American armies invade Italy
1944	D-day invasion of France; R. A. Butler's Education Act
1945	End of war in Europe (8 May) and in Far East (15 August); general election: massive Labour victory and Clement Attlee becomes prime minister
1947	Coal and other industries nationalized; convertibility crisis; transfer of power to independent India, Pakistan, and Burma
1948	Bevan launches National Health Service

1949	NATO founded; devaluation of the pound by Stafford Cripps
1950	General election: Labour retains power by narrow majority; outbreak of war in Korea
1951	Festival of Britain; general election: Conservatives defeat Labour, and Churchill again becomes prime minister
1952	Death of King George VI; Queen Elizabeth II proclaimed
1954	British troops withdraw from Egypt
1955	Eden becomes prime minister; general election won by Conservatives
1956	Anglo-French invasion of Suez, followed by withdrawal
1957	Anthony Eden resigns; Harold Macmillan becomes prime minister
1959	General election: Conservatives win with larger majority
1963	French veto Britain's application to join the European Common Market; test-ban treaty in Moscow limits nuclear testing; Alec Douglas-Home succeeds Macmillan as prime minister
1964	General election: Labour under Harold Wilson win narrow majority
1966	General election: Labour win with much larger majority
1967	Devaluation of the pound
1968	Restriction of Commonwealth immigration
1970	General election: Conservatives under Edward Heath returned to office
1972	National miners' strike; Stormont government abolished in Northern Ireland
1973	Britain enters European Common Market
1974	National miners' strike; two general elections: Labour under Wilson win both with narrow majorities
1975	Popular referendum confirms British membership of the Common Market
1976	Economic crisis: Britain obtains help from International Monetary Fund
1979	Devolution referendums in Wales and Scotland; general

	election: Conservatives under Margaret Thatcher returned to office; independence granted to Zimbabwe (Rhodesia)
1980	Britain becomes self-sufficient in North Sea oil
1981	Social Democratic Party founded
1982	Britain defeats Argentina in war over the Falkland Islands
1983	General election: Thatcher's Conservative government returned with massive majority; Cruise missiles installed
1984	Miners' strike
1985	Miners' strike ends after a year; Anglo-Irish Hillsborough Agreement signed
1986	Channel Tunnel treaty signed; 'Big Bang' in Stock Exchange
1987	General election: Thatcher's Conservative government again returned with a majority of over 100; Stock Exchange collapse in the autumn
1989	Poll tax introduced first in Scotland
1990	Britain joins Exchange Rate Mechanism (ERM); resignation of Thatcher; John Major becomes prime minister
1991	Gulf War against Iraq
1992	Conservatives unexpectedly retain power at general election; 'Black Wednesday': Britain leaves the ERM
1994	IRA declares cease-fire in Northern Ireland
1996	Prince Charles and Princess Diana divorce
1997	Labour wins general election with majority of 179: Tony Blair becomes prime minister; death of Princess Diana in car crash in Paris; Scotland and Wales vote for devolution in referendums; Britain withdraws from Hong Kong
1998	Good Friday agreement in Northern Ireland
1999	Economic and Monetary Union (EMU) begins (1 January), without Britain; first elections for Scottish Parliament and Welsh Assembly; Northern Ireland Assembly meets; hereditary peers' seats in the House of Lords abolished
2000	Millennium Dome opens; first elected mayor of London

Prime Ministers 1914–2000

(Herbert Henry Asquith	*Apr. 1908)*
David Lloyd George	Dec. 1916
Andrew Bonar Law	Oct. 1922
Stanley Baldwin	May 1923
James Ramsay MacDonald	Jan. 1924
Stanley Baldwin	Nov. 1924
James Ramsay MacDonald	June 1929
Stanley Baldwin	June 1935
Neville Chamberlain	May 1937
Winston Churchill	May 1940
Clement Attlee	July 1945
Winston Churchill	Oct. 1951
Sir Anthony Eden	Apr. 1955
Harold Macmillan	Jan. 1957
Sir Alec Douglas-Home	Oct. 1963
Harold Wilson	Oct. 1964
Edward Heath	June 1970
Harold Wilson	Mar. 1974
James Callaghan	Apr. 1976
Margaret Thatcher	May 1979
John Major	Nov. 1990
Tony Blair	May 1997

Index

Page numbers in *italics* refer to illustrations or captions. There may also be textual references on the same page.

A

Abyssinia 40
Addison, Dr Christopher, Viscount (1869–1951) 16, 26, *62*
Africa 52, 69, 85–6; *see also* North Africa; South Africa
agriculture 8, 27, 98
Aldermaston *see* Nuclear Disarmament
Allenby, Field Marshal Edmund, 1st Viscount (1861–1936) 6
Anderson, Sir John, Viscount Waverley (1882–1958) 54
Anglicans *see* Church of England
architecture 21, 38–9, 66–7, 90, 102; *see also* housing
army 3, *4*, 10–11
Arnhem, battle of 51
Arsenal Football Club 36
Arts Council 66
arts, visual 21–2, 38, 56
Asquith, Herbert Henry, Earl (1852–1928) 2, 8, 10–11, 14
Association Football 36, 64, 74
Astor, Waldorf, Viscount (1879–1952) and Nancy, Lady (1879–1964) 40

B

Attlee, Clement Richard (1883–1967) 58, 61, *62*, 65, 69, 103–4
Auchinleck, Field Marshal Sir Claude (1884–1981) 50
Auden, Wystan Hugh (1907–73) 37, 41
Austin, Herbert, Baron (1866–1941) 27, *27*
Australia, Commonwealth of 13, 49, 51
Avon, earl of *see* Eden

Bad Godesberg 42
Bairnsfather, Bruce 6
Baker, Sir Herbert (1862–1946) 13
Baldwin, Stanley, Earl (1867–1947) 13, 20, 24, 26, 29, 33, 40
Barlow report (1940) 54
Bax, Arnold (1883–1953) 38
BBC 23–4, 25, 26, 57, 67, 90
Beatles, the 74, 102
Beatty, Admiral David, Earl (1871–1936) 6
Beaverbrook, Max Aitken, Baron (1879–1964) 48
Beckett, Samuel (1906–89) 66
Belfast 28, 77, 97, 105
Belgium 2, 9, 47
Bell, Vanessa (1879–1961) 22
Benn, Anthony Wedgwood (b. 1925) 87, 92
Berchtesgaden 42
Best, George (b. 1946) 73–4
Betjeman, John (1906–84) 35

betting 102

Bevan, Aneurin (1897–1960) 55, 62–3

Beveridge report 53–4, 58, 62

Beveridge, Sir William (1879–1963) 8, 53–4, 58

Bevin, Ernest (1881–1955) 40, 42, 58, 60, 62

Blair, Tony (b. 1952) 103–6, 108

'Bloomsbury group' 21–2, 37

Blyton, Enid (1897–1968) 68

Bonar Law see Law

Bradley, General Omar Nelson (1893–1983) 50

Bretton Woods agreement 54

Bristol, St Paul's district 83

Britten, Benjamin (1913–76) 56, 66

broadcasting 26, 67; see also BBC

Butler, Richard Austen, Baron (1902–82) 59, 65; Education Act (1944) 57

C

Callaghan, Leonard James (b. 1912) 80, 103

Cambridge University 23, 24, 37

Canada 13, 49

car industry 26, 27, 36

Cardiff 90

Carson, Sir Edward, Baron (1854–1935) 11

Cary, Joyce (1888–1957) 65

Cavell, Edith (1865–1915) 9

Central African Federation 69

Chamberlain, Neville (1869–1940) 13, 26, 29, 34, 41–4, 47, 94

Channel Tunnel 85, 88, 101

Chapman, Herbert (1878–1934) 36

Charles, Prince (b. 1948) 100, 108

Church of England 23–4, 108; see also Prayer Book

Churchill, Winston Leonard Spencer (1874–1965) 5, 11, 25, 28, 31, 39, 40, 42, 43–4, 48–52, 58, 59, 65, 69

cinema 29, 56, 67, 68, 101, 102

Citrine, Walter McLennan, Viscount (1887–1983) 42, 58

Clarke, Kenneth (b. 1940) 97

Cliveden (Bucks.) 40

CND see Nuclear Disarmament

coal-mining 18, 24–5, 78, 87

Collins, Michael (1890–1922) 14, 17

colonies see Empire

Common Wealth Party 59

Commonwealth see Empire

Conservative Party 10, 12–15, 18, 33–4, 40, 47, 60, 65, 71, 77, 80, 85–7, 91–7 passim, 98–100, 104; see also Tories

Cook, Arthur James (1883–1931) 25

Corn Production Act (1917) 8

Coward, Noël (1899–1973) 22

Crick, Francis Harry (b. 1916) 69

Cripps, Sir Stafford (1889–1952) 40, 60, 62

Czechoslovakia 42–3

D

Daily Mirror 53
Dalton, Hugh, Baron (1887–1962)
 58–9, 60, *62*
Dardanelles expedition (1915) 5
Davidson, Randall Thomas,
 archbishop of Canterbury
 (1848–1930) 23
Day-Lewis, Cecil (1904–72) 37
de Gaulle, President Charles
 (1890–1970) 73
de Valera, Eamon (1882–1975) 14,
 49
Delius, Frederick (1862–1934) 38
Derby scheme *4*
Devonport, Hudson Ewbanke
 Kearley, 1st Viscount
 (1856–1934) 8
Diana, Princess (1961–97) 100,
 107, 108, *109*
Dillon, John (1851–1927) 14
Dimbleby, Richard (1913–65) 57
Dissent 23
Distribution of Industry Act
 (1945) 54
Douglas-Home, Sir Alexander
 Frederick, Baron (1903–95) 65
drama 21–2, 37, 65–6
Dunkirk evacuation 47–8
Durrell, Lawrence (1912–90) 65

E

East Anglia 88
Eden, Robert Anthony, 1st earl of
 Avon (1897–1977) 42, 65, 69–
 70

education 8, 37, 57, 63; *see also*
 universities
Edward VIII (duke of Windsor,
 1894–1972) 33–4, 37
Eisenhower, General Dwight
 David (1890–1969) 51
El Alamein 50
Elgar, Sir Edward (1857–1934) 21,
 31, *38*
Eliot, Thomas Stearns
 (1888–1963) 21, 37
Elizabeth II (b. 1926) 100, 108
Empire and Commonwealth
 13–14, 49–52, 69–73, *70*; *see
 also under individual countries*
energy 79, 88, *89*
European Common Market/
 European Community 73,
 84–5, 96–9, 105, 106
European Exchange Rate
 Mechanism 85, 96
evacuation *46*, 53

F

Falkland Islands 86–7, 95
Festival of Britain 64–5
film *see* cinema
First World War 1–14, *19*
Fisher, H. A. L., Education Act
 (1918) 8
Fitzgerald, Garret (b. 1926) 82
Fleming, Sir Alexander
 (1881–1955) 69
Florey, Howard, Baron
 (1898–1968) 69
Foot, Michael (b. 1913) 43–4

Forster, Edward Morgan
(1879–1970) 21
Franco, General Francisco
(1892–1975) 40–1
free trade 34
French, Field Marshal Sir John,
Earl (1852–1925) 6
Fry, Roger (1866–1934) 22

G

Gaitskell, Hugh T. N. (1906–63)
65
Gandhi, Mahatma (1869–1948)
39
Geddes, Sir Eric (1875–1937) 8
General Strike (1926) 24–6
George V (1856–1936) 29, 37
Germany 2–6, 16, 18, 36, 39–52,
46, 59, 98; *see also* First World
War; Second World War
Grace, William Gilbert
(1848–1915) 30
Graf Spee, sinking of 45
Grant, Duncan (1885–1978) 22
Graves, Robert (1895–1985) 6
Greece 50
Greene, Graham (1904–91) 38
Greenwood, Arthur (1880–1954)
43, 58–9, *62*
Greenwood, Walter (1903–74)
35
Griffith, Arthur (1872–1922) 17
Griffiths, James (1890–1975)
60
Gulf War (1991) 95, 99

H

Haig, Field Marshal Sir Douglas,
Earl (1861–1928) 5, 6
Handley, Tommy (1892–1949) 57
Hardie, James Keir (1856–1915)
103
Hardy, Thomas (1840–1928) 21, 31
Heath, Edward (b. 1916) 77
Henderson, Sir Nevile
(1882–1942) 41
Hepworth, Barbara (1903–75) 38
Heseltine, Michael (b. 1933) 94
Hess, Dame Myra (1890–1965) 56
Hiroshima 51–2
Hitler, Adolf (1883–1945) 40–4,
48–9, 51
Hoare, Sir Samuel, Viscount
Templewood (1880–1959) 39,
43
Hobbs, Jack (1883–1963) 29–30,
73–4
Holden, Charles Henry
(1875–1960) 38
Holst, Gustav (1874–1934) 38
Home *see* Douglas-Home
home guard 47–8
Hong Kong 85
Hopkinson, Tom (1905–90) 53
housing 8–9, 16, 26, 36, 62
Hutton, Will (b. 1950) 100

I

India 1, 13, 14, 33, 51, 69
industry 32, 34–5, 36, 53–4; *see
also* car industry; steel
industry

IRA 77, 81–2
Ireland 1, 14, 15, 17, 39, 82, 97, 105–6; *see also* Northern Ireland
Italy 40–1, 49–50

J

Japan 49, 50–1
Jarrow 28, 54, 60
Jenkins, Roy (b. 1920) 74
Jones, Lewis (1899–1939) 35
Jones, Thomas (1870–1955) 35
Joyce, James (1882–1941) 21
Jutland, battle of (1916) 5

K

Keynes, John Maynard (1883–1946) 18–20, 19, 22, 28, 39, 54, 58, 77, 87
Kinnock, Neil (b. 1942) 91, 94, 96, 102–3
Kipling, Rudyard (1865–1936) 21, 31, 86

L

Labour Party 8, 11, 12–13, 15, 18, 20, 25, 31, 32–3, 42, 43, 47, 55, 58–60, 61–5, 71–2, 74, 80, 85, 87–8, 91–3, 96–8, 102–6
Lamont, Norman (b. 1942) 96–7
land tenure 27–8
Lang, Cosmo Gordon, archbishop of Canterbury (1864–1945) 23

Lansdowne, Henry Charles Keith, 5th marquess of (1845–1927) 3
Laski, Harold (1893–1950) 71–2
Law, Andrew Bonar (1858–1923) 11, 20
Lawrence, David Herbert (1885–1930) 21
Lawrence, Thomas Edward ('of Arabia', 1888–1935) 14
Lawson, Nigel (b. 1932) 93
League of Nations 40
Leeds 90
Liberal Party 2, 8, 10–11, 16, 17, 33, 58
Lindemann, Frederick, Viscount Cherwell (1886–1957) 41
Lipton, Sir Thomas (1850–1931) 31
literature 5, 21–2, 37–8, 56, 65–6, 90; *see also* drama
Liverpool, Toxteth 83
Lloyd George, David, Earl (1863–1945) 1, 2, 5, 7, 8, 10, 11–20, 31, 32, 39, 42, 47, 94, 95
local government 93
London 1, 2, 16, 20, 34, 35, 36, 38–9, 48, 53, 56, 66, 72, 82–3, 88, 90, 97, 100–1, 102, 109
Londonderry 77
Londonderry, Edith Helen, marchioness of (1879–1959) 31
Loos 4–5
Lutyens, Sir Edwin (1869–1944) 6, 13, 21, 24
Lynn, Vera (b. 1917) 57

M

Maastricht Treaty (1990) 95, 97, 98

MacDonald, James Ramsay (1866–1937) 8, 12, 20, 31, 33

Mackintosh, Charles Rennie (1868–1928) 38

Maclay, Sir Joseph (1857–1951) 8

Macmillan, Harold (1894–1986) 65, 71, 74

MacNeice, Louis (1907–63) 37

Major, John (b. 1943) 95–101 *passim*, 103, 105

Malawi 69

Malaya 51

Manchester 66

McKenna, Reginald (1863–1943) 11

Medical Research Council 9

Merthyr Tydfil (Glam.) 28

millennium 108, 109

minorities, ethnic 76–7, 82–3, 101

Mitterrand, François (1916–96) 85

monarchy 33, 37, 100, 109

Mons 2

Montgomery, Field Marshal Bernard, Viscount (1887–1976) 50, 51

Moore, George Edward (1873–1958) 22

Moore, Henry (1898–1986) 38, 55, 56

Morris, William, Viscount Nuffield (1877–1963) 26, 27

Morrison, Herbert, Baron (1888–1965) 58, 60, *62*

Mosley, Sir Oswald (1896–1980) 33

Mountbatten, Louis, Earl Mountbatten of Burma (1900–79) 81–2

Moynihan, Daniel Patrick (b. 1927) 71

Munich agreement (1938) 41

Murdoch, Iris (1919–99) 65

music 38, 56, 66, 74, 90

music-hall 29

N

Nagasaki 51–2

Nash, Paul (1889–1946) 22, 38

Nassau agreements 72–3

National Debt 16–17

National Front 92

National Government (1931–40) 33–47 *passsim*

National Health Service 54, 62, 93, 105

National Lottery 102

NATO 72, 84

navy and naval warfare 39, 45, 48–9

Netherlands 47

New Delhi 13

New Zealand 13, 49, 51

Nicholson, Ben (1894–1982) 22

North Africa 50

Northern Ireland 65, 77, 81–2, 92, 97, 105, 106; *see also* Ireland

Northern Rhodesia *see* Zambia

Norway 47

Nossiter, Bernard D. 91

Nuclear Disarmament,
    Campaign for 74, 75, 84

Nyasaland *see* Malawi

O

Orwell, George (Eric Blair,
    1903–50) 26, 35, 41, 52

Osborne, John (1929–94) 66

Ottawa Conference (1932) 34

Owen, Frank (1905–79) 44

Owen, Wilfred (1893–1918) 5

Oxford University 23, 24, 37, 83,
    103

P

Paisley, Ian R. K. (b. 1926) 81

Pankhurst, Christabel
    (1880–1958) 9

Pankhurst, Emmeline
    (1858–1928) 9

Pankhurst, Sylvia (1882–1960) 9

Parliament 10–11, 37, 47, 86, 99,
    106, 110

Passchendaele 5–6

Pearl Harbor 49

Percival, General A. E.
    (1887–1966) 51

'permissive society' 74

Pick, Frank (1878–1941) 38

Picture Post 53

Pinter, Harold (b. 1930) 66

Piper, John (1903–92) 56

Plaid Cymru 21, 76

Poland 43–4

poll tax 93, 95, 104

poor relief 29; *see also* poverty

population 26, 80; migration
    34–5

poverty 29, 36, 82, 101

Powell, J. Enoch (1912–98) 77

Prayer Book 23

prices *see* wages

Priestley, John Boynton
    (1894–1984) 53

public health 9; *see also*
    National Health Service

Q

Quakers 35

R

radicalism 59, 92

Redmond, John (1856–1918) 14

Redwood, John (b. 1951) 99

religion 108; Christianity 23–4;
    see also Church of England

Rhondda, David Alfred Thomas,
    Viscount (1856–1918) 8

Robey, George (1869–1954) 29

Roman Catholicism 23

Rosenberg, Isaac (1890–1918) 5

Rowntree, Seebohm (1871–1954)
    8

Royal Academy 39

Royal Air Force 41, 48

Russell, Bertrand, Earl
    (1872–1970) 52

Russia 43–4, 49, 50, 59; Bolshevik
    revolution 3, 12

S

Saddam Hussein 95
Salisbury, James, 4th marquess of (1861–1947) 8
Sassoon, Siegfried (1886–1967) 6
science and technology 88; see also industry
Schoenberg, Arnold (1874–1951) 38
Scotland 3, 7, 21, 23, 24, 28, 35, 43, 63, 76, 77, 81, 82, 92, 104, 105, 106, 108, 109
SEATO 72
Second World War 45–60 passim
Shaw, George Bernard (1856–1950) 21, 33
Shaw, Richard Norman (1831–1912) 38
Shinwell, Emanuel (1884–1986) 55
Simon, Sir John, Viscount (1873–1954) 11, 43
Simpson, Wallis, duchess of Windsor (1896–1986) 34
Singapore 39, 51
Sinn Fein 14, 15, 17, 77, 97, 105
Slough (Bucks.) 35
Smith, John (1938–94) 103
Smuts, Field Marshal Jan Christian (1870–1950) 13
Social Democratic Party 87–8, 91
social stability 100–1
Somme, battle of the (1916) 5
South Africa 13, 49
Southern Rhodesia see Zimbabwe

Soviet Union see Russia
Spain 41, 44, 60, 73, 76, 85; Civil War 40–1
Spencer, Stanley (1891–1959) 38
Spender, Stephen (1909–95) 37
Spice Girls 102
steel industry 34, 61–2, 81
Stock Exchange 88–90
Strachey, Lytton (1880–1932) 22
Stravinsky, Igor (1882–1971) 38
Sudetenland 42
Suez Canal 49–50, 70, 71
Sutherland, Graham (1903–80) 56

T

Tawney, Richard Henry (1880–1962) 28, 71–2
technology see science
television 67–8, 83, 102, 110
Thatcher, Margaret (b. 1925) 82, 85, 87, 90, 91–4, 104
'Thatcherism' 93
theatre see drama
Thomas, Dylan (1914–53) 66
Tippett, Sir Michael K. (1905–98) 56
Tizard, Sir Henry (1885–1959) 41
Tobruk 50
towns and town life 26–9, 35–6, 54, 66, 88, 96, 102, 109; suburbs 26
trade unions 8, 12, 57–8, 65, 80–1, 83; strikes 1, 7, 18,

24-6, 58, 65, 78, 80, 83, 87;
    TUC 2, 25, 58
Treasury Agreement (1915) 7

U

unemployment 18, 28, 32, 33, 65,
    77-8, 80-1, 91
Union of Democratic Control 3
United States of America 32, 33,
    37, 49, 50-2, 63, 66, 68,
    69-72 *passim*, 76, 83, 84, 86,
    91, 95, 99, 103, 109
universities 74-6, 90; *see also*
    Cambridge University; Oxford
    University
Utthwatt report (1942) 54

V

Vaughan-Thomas, Wynford
    (1908-87) 57
Vaughan Williams, Ralph
    (1872-1958) 38
Versailles, treaty of (1919) 18, 40
'Vicky' (Victor Weisz, 1913-66)
    65
Voysey, Charles Francis Annesley
    (1857-1941) 38

W

wages and prices 8, 26, 64-5, 68,
    73, 78, 79-81, 84, 96, 104
Wales 3, 7, 14, 21, 23, 25, 28, 35,
    43, 53, 55, 57, 58, 76, 77, 82,
    87, 92, 104, 106, 110
Walton, Sir William (1902-83) 66
war, attitudes to 3-4, 5-6, 19,
    39-44, 52, 74-6, 84, 86-7

Watson, James Dewey (b. 1928)
    69
Waugh, Evelyn (1903-66) 38, 45
Wavell, Field Marshal Archibald
    P., Earl (1883-1950) 50
Webb, Sidney (Baron Passfield)
    (1859-1947) and Beatrice
    (1858-1943) 8, 33
Weisz, Victor *see* 'Vicky'
welfare state 58, 61-5, 80, 103-4
Wells, Herbert George
    (1866-1946) 33
Wigan 28
Wilkinson, Ellen (1891-1947) 54,
    62
Wilson, Angus (1913-91) 65
Wilson, Colin (b. 1931) 66
Wilson, Sir Harold (1916-95) 65,
    76, 80
Wilson, Sir Horace (1882-1972)
    41
Wingate, Major-General Orde
    (1903-44) 51
women in society 9, 22, 92, 101
Wood, Sir Henry Joseph
    (1869-1944) 39
Wood, Sir Kingsley (1881-1943)
    54
Woolf, Virginia (1882-1941) 21
working class 26-30, 57-8, 73-4

Y

Ypres 2

Z

Zambia 69
Zimbabwe 85-6

Expand your collection of
VERY SHORT INTRODUCTIONS

1. Classics
2. Music
3. Buddhism
4. Literary Theory
5. Hinduism
6. Psychology
7. Islam
8. Politics
9. Theology
10. Archaeology
11. Judaism
12. Sociology
13. The Koran
14. The Bible
15. Social and Cultural Anthropology
16. History
17. Roman Britain
18. The Anglo-Saxon Age
19. Medieval Britain
20. The Tudors
21. Stuart Britain
22. Eighteenth-Century Britain
23. Nineteenth-Century Britain
24. Twentieth-Century Britain
25. Heidegger
26. Ancient Philosophy
27. Socrates
28. Marx
29. Logic
30. Descartes
31. Machiavelli
32. Aristotle
33. Hume
34. Nietzsche
35. Darwin
36. The European Union
37. Gandhi
38. Augustine
39. Intelligence
40. Jung
41. Buddha
42. Paul
43. Continental Philosophy
44. Galileo
45. Freud
46. Wittgenstein
47. Indian Philosophy
48. Rousseau
49. Hegel
50. Kant
51. Cosmology
52. Drugs
53. Russian Literature
54. The French Revolution
55. Philosophy
56. Barthes
57. Animal Rights
58. Kierkegaard
59. Russell
60. Shakespeare
61. Clausewitz
62. Schopenhauer
63. The Russian Revolution
64. Hobbes
65. World Music
66. Mathematics
67. Philosophy of Science
68. Cryptography
69. Quantum Theory
70. Spinoza

71. Choice Theory
72. Architecture
73. Poststructuralism
74. Postmodernism
75. Democracy
76. Empire
77. Fascism
78. Terrorism
79. Plato
80. Ethics
81. Emotion
82. Northern Ireland
83. Art Theory
84. Locke
85. Modern Ireland
86. Globalization
87. Cold War
88. The History of Astronomy
89. Schizophrenia
90. The Earth
91. Engels
92. British Politics
93. Linguistics
94. The Celts
95. Ideology
96. Prehistory
97. Political Philosophy
98. Postcolonialism
99. Atheism
100. Evolution
101. Molecules
102. Art History
103. Presocratic Philosophy
104. The Elements
105. Dada and Surrealism
106. Egyptian Myth
107. Christian Art

Visit the
VERY SHORT INTRODUCTIONS
Web site

www.oup.co.uk/vsi

➤ **Information** about all published titles

➤ News of **forthcoming books**

➤ **Extracts** from the books, including titles not yet published

➤ **Reviews** and views

➤ **Links** to other **web sites** and main OUP web page

➤ Information about **VSIs in translation**

➤ **Contact** the editors

➤ **Order** other **VSIs** on-line